# COPING
# WITH
# CHANGE

I have often recommended Walt Kaiser's *Ecclesiastes: Total Life* to students who've asked for help on this tantalizing biblical book. Now Dr. Kaiser has given us *Coping with Change*. The 'bones' are much the same but the whole has been updated and much expanded. Perhaps the most helpful feature of Kaiser's treatment is that he believes the book has a discernible plan and a traceable argument and that Qoheleth was *not* a cynical old goat who drank Drano or vinegar for breakfast. That makes a difference in the way you understand Ecclesiastes. Buy your own copy and find out how.

Dale Ralph Davis
Well-respected author and Bible expositor, rural Tennessee

Few things are less popular today than ancient wisdom. Few things are more needed. Walt Kaiser's *Coping with Change* walks us through the book of Ecclesiastes, functioning like a scholarly tour guide through the mind of a man who had seen and done and achieved it all--and has realized that everything is a "mist" without God. This is a profound meditation on the wisest of books; one is tempted, in fact, to call Kaiser Solomonic, and his textual musings elegantly prepare us to discover that the divine glory Solomon saw only dimly has now shone fully in the face of Jesus Christ, who is the very radiance of God.

Owen Strachan
Assistant Professor of Christian Theology and Church History,
Boyce College, Louisville, Kentucky
co-author, *Essential Edwards Collection*

Ecclesiastes is a wisdom writing from ancient Israel but there is no book more relevant for our postmodern world today. Dr. Walter Kaiser, one of our best biblical scholars, has given us a lively commentary on this part of God's Word, one that will help us face today's changing world with integrity and faithfulness.

Timothy George
Founding Dean of Beeson Divinity School of Samford University and the General Editor of the Reformation Commentary on Scripture, Birmingham, Alabama

# COPING WITH CHANGE

## ECCLESIASTES

WALTER C. KAISER, JR.

CHRISTIAN
FOCUS

Walter C. Kaiser, Jr., Ph.D., is the Colman M. Mockler distinguished Professor of Old Testament and President Emeritus of Gordon-Conwell Theological Seminary, Massachusetts. He has written extensively in theological journals and has authored a host of books, including *Revive Us Again* and *Grief and Pain in the Plan of God*. Dr. Kaiser and his wife, Marge live in Cedar Grove, Wisconsin have four adult children and seven grandchildren.

Copyright © Walter C. Kaiser, Jr. 2013

paperback ISBN 978-1-78191-062-7
epub ISBN 978-1-78191-223-2
mobi ISBN 978-1-78191-225-6

10 9 8 7 6 5 4 3 2 1

Published in 2013
by
Christian Focus Publications, Ltd
Geanies House, Fearn,
Ross-shire, IV20 1TW, Scotland
www.christianfocus.com

Cover design
by
DUFI-ART.com

Printed by
Bell and Bain, Glasgow

MIX
Paper from
responsible sources
FSC® C007785

# CONTENTS

# PREFACE

To the twenty-first century "man or woman in the street," life looks more like a "puzzle"—with "change" being so constant that it tends to dominate contemporary thinking more than anything else today. Most persons today feel that they, like their culture, have become plastic-like and subject to constant change and redefinition. For just as plastic now symbolizes the chief achievement of research, technocracy, and the massive sales of the distribution agencies in our day, so also people feel themselves to be the fruit of sociological research and constant manipulation by economic, political, social, and religious technocracies—bent to whatever shape life and society feels it would like to mold or change persons, institutions, society, and morals to today.

For many, life has lost its zip. There is no joy in town—or anywhere else, not because our hero has struck out in baseball, but because life just doesn't seem to be any fun anymore. All our talk about morality, it is claimed, only makes one feel cheap, commercial, dead, and machine-like, for why should anyone care any longer? The basic worth and dignity of modern men and women are repeatedly denied when their humanity is deliberately overlooked and they are equated with the brute animals and, worse still, treated as if they were merely machines. All the while, everything within those same persons cries out for a larger view of the entirety of life and for some kind of stability and perspective from which to evaluate all that seems to be in constant flux and change.

Meanwhile, our universe seems to grow increasingly silent as more and more turn away from the God who made them and who maintains the universe. Twenty-first century mortals are gripped by an inexplicable loneliness. Is there no one home in the universe? Are we really "Home Alone"? If it could only be true that there was life on other planets, we might not feel so alone, whimper some postmoderns of our day, now that so many refuse to recognize God in our own universe. Surely if God is dead, as many depersonalized theologians said in the 1960s (the "God is Dead theologians"), echoing each other in their new, faceless roles, there must be someone or something else out there. There has to be, or we are stuck! We are "Home Alone"!

But no, the agony, dread, nothingness, and boredom are worse than anyone had imagined. Not only is loneliness a current symptom; so are boredom and the emptiness of life without God! Truth with a capital "T" continues to disappear in Western civilization, almost in direct proportion to the disappearance of God from modern thought. "All is relative" now, goes the slogan— and ironically that statement itself is the only absolute left. Moreover, change is the only constant for many in our day, so all is relative. "All is absolutely relative!" some argue contradictorily!

The best illustration of what relativity means was forcefully brought to my attention as I attended a "Danforth Teacher Study Grant Seminar" in 1961, just before entering my doctor of philosophy (Ph.D.) studies at Brandeis University in Waltham, Massachusetts. During one of the week-long summer seminars required for all grant-recipients, one of the fellow award-winners of the Danforth Teacher Study Grants, a liberal arts college art teacher (from a presumed Christian college no less), was asked to explain one of his oil paintings (which the foundation had generously shipped to the seminars along with numerous other paintings), as five other artists who preceded him had done for the conference. I will never forget his candor as he responded to a question about what it was that he had intended to communicate in one of his expressionist paintings with its swirls of dark browns, blacks, greens, and grays covering the canvas. He said, "Well, I will tell you this: when I finished painting this picture, I stepped back, and it didn't say anything to me. Then," he continued, "I turned the painting on its side, and still it didn't *say* anything to me." I certainly followed him up to that point, for I too had not been able to make heads or tails out of what he had intended in this work. To my amazement, he concluded by saying, "So, I turned the picture upside down, and *that* is what I wanted to say! So that is how I show the picture now." He had finished the painting, and he was now trying to assess what it was that he had done! He had painted it, apparently, upside down!

Only then did I fully begin to grasp what a terrific price was to be paid by postmodern Western men and women for the loss of the standard of truth and personal dignity in a world without God. For the picture (created by a valuable, thinking, and creative artist, who was made in the image of God) became the father of the painter. He, the creator of the painting, became shaped and molded by his own creation! In his search for meaning, value, beauty, and the joy of the aesthetic, he was consumed and replaced by his own production; the thing usurped the place of a mortal made in the image of God!

Ecclesiastes is the best news around for such baffled and confused postmodern men and women. It is the book for persons who want to live again—now. It is the working person's book: it answers the residual boredom and loneliness of postmodernity, especially for those who are tired of the routine of joylessly eating, drinking, and earning a paycheck—but with no sense of any enjoyment in the whole process, or even of where any of it comes from, much less with what any of it means!

Ecclesiastes is also the thinking person's book. Its author knew that the reader is haunted by the questions: What does a person get for all his or her toil and struggles in life? Who am I, anyway? What is the meaning of this treadmill called life? Why is there so much change and why are there so few points of reference, or any solid ground, where I can plant my feet, from which I can view the whole of life? Should I be "worldlier than thou" or should I adopt a "holier than thou" position? Or is there a third alternative that is simultaneously world-accepting and God-honoring?

Ecclesiastes has as its central concern that basic hunger of mortals to see how the wholeness of life fits into a meaningful pattern where its purpose and plan is owned and directed by God. Can this current age with so much brutality, injustice, and lack of cohesiveness come to be at once accepted, enjoyed, and understood to fit in any way into the divine plan and purpose for life? And if the same laws and plans of the omnipotent God apply to all reality, why does there often seem to be so little evidence of the positive sides of the divine plan in effect? Where are the goodness and joy of life evident in the constant change and transitions of a life that so often puzzles us? Where is the sovereign direction of a wise, powerful, and good God when suffering Christians need Him most and seemingly He is not there?

Ecclesiastes was written to give perspective and some practical advice on the above questions. It is in many ways a companion book to Job. Yet in other ways it is also a book of very unusual, but desperately needed, messages, especially for our day. It is no wonder that of all the books of the Bible read by contemporary college and university students, this is the one that, more often than not, "turns them on" the most. There is a good reason for that: it was written for persons just like them, and, in fact, for persons just like all of us who are afflicted with the postmodern, Western trends and diagnoses.

My prayer is that the Living God, who delights in restoring the joy of this life, and the joy of living significantly, for those who would otherwise be little more than empty, plastic men and women of the twenty-first century, will use Ecclesiastes and this revised set of studies to provide a biblical definition of the relationship between Christ and culture. The need is as great for many believers who are held in a postmodern, Western, cultural, and consumerist captivity, as it is for many unbelievers who are similarly saddled with ideas that are hostile to their image-bearing of God and who likewise swim in the technological and non-theistic eddies of our day and unthinkingly adopt pagan solutions to the questions of life and truth.

One final word before you open the text of Scripture and follow the comments in the pages that follow. In addition to sincerely acknowledging my gratitude to all my students during the past fifty years or so for the many happy hours spent in probing some of the questions dealt with in Ecclesiastes in all sorts of contexts and subjects, I must thank those who originally typed the earlier edition of this manuscript in its first edition in 1978 with the same joy and wholehearted involvement as that taught in the book of Ecclesiastes. My thanks go to Mrs. Jenny Wiers, Mrs. Kathy Wiggins, and Mrs. Jan Olander. Ecclesiastes pointedly reminds me that my wife is a gift from God, and therefore I also cheerfully acknowledge her encouragement and willingness to continue to fill in the gaps while I was occupied with the hours of rewriting and extended research. That state of affairs she has continued through a half-century of my teaching and preaching—a real indoor record to say the least!

I have included in this new edition my own translation of Ecclesiastes, since the meaning of this book, more than perhaps any other book of the Bible, is affected by the translator's presuppositions.

# INTRODUCTION

## THE UNITY OF THE BOOK

No book of the Bible has been so maligned, and so misunderstood, as the Old Testament book of Ecclesiastes. The most frequent assessment of the book is summed up in such negative terms as nihilistic, pessimistic, fatalistic, skeptical, cynical, materialistic, experimental, and the like. It was none other than Ernest Renan (the French humanist and historian of religion, 1823-92) who remarked with some insight and wit that

> Ecclesiastes passed formerly as the most obscure book of the Bible. This is only the opinion of theologians, and in reality it is completely false. The book as a whole is very clear; only theologians had a major interest to find it obscure.[1]

Few books in the world, even those of the Bible, have had as bewildering an array of interpretations as Ecclesiastes—even by evangelical interpreters! For example, to quote

---

1    Ernest Renan, *L'Ecclésiaste: traduit de l'hebreu avec une étude sur l'âge et le caractère du livre*. Trans. Eric S. Christianson. (Paris: Anciennes Maison Michel Levy Frères, 1882), p. 15.

a non-evangelical extreme, F. Zimmermann[2] argued that this book came from a highly neurotic, impotent bureaucrat with homosexual tendencies—an assessment without any basis in fact. Even the evangelical author David Hubbard began his study of this book by saying, "Few Old Testament writings have produced such a flurry of opinions as to how they should be read, and what they mean, as Ecclesiastes.... Trying to puzzle out the major themes of his message is a task tantalizing, frustrating, and important."[3]

Even though, as a whole, the book is for almost all readers and interpreters a nightmare when it comes to locating what the overall purpose and teaching is, it exists as a storehouse of memorable citations such as the following:

Vanity of vanities! All is vanity. (Eccles. 1:2, ESV)

There is nothing new under the sun, (1:9)

There is a time for everything, and a season for every activity under heaven, (3:1, NIV)

A cord of three strands is not quickly broken, (4:12)

Cast your bread upon the waters, for after many days you will find it again, (11:1)

Remember now your Creator in the days of your youth, (12:1, NKJV)

and

Of making many books there is no end. (12:12)

---

2    F. Zimmermann, *The Inner World of Qoheleth* (New York, KTAV, 1973, pp. 1-97), as reported in Duane A. Garrett, *The New American Commentary* (Nashville, TN: 1993), vol. 14, p. 271, n88.

3    David A. Hubbard, *The Communicator's Commentary: Ecclesiastes, Song of Solomon* (Dallas, TX: Word Books, 1991), p. 19.

Yet despite these and many other well-known aphorisms from the book, its seeming negativism is particularly troubling to many devout readers and interpreters of Scripture.

But certainly the so-called negative estimates of many interpreters reflect a superficial or an atomistic reading of the book, for if Ecclesiastes is a unit, it also expresses an impressive list of positive ethical and spiritual injunctions, not to mention the conclusion that the epilogue comes to. For instance, there are those repeated exhortations to: (1) "fear God" (3:14; 5:7; 7:18; 8:12-13 [three times]; 12:13); (2) receive all the "good" things of life as a "gift from God" (2:24-26; 5:18-19; 8:15; 9:7-9); (3) reflect on the fact that God will "judge the righteous and the wicked" (3:17; 8:12-13; 11:9; 12:7b; 12:14); and (4) remember that God presently reviews the quality of every man's lifestyle (3:15b; 5:6b; 7:29; 8:5; 8:13; 11:9b; 12:1). These statements must be given as full a play in interpreting the book as any of the other statements found in it as well.

But pointing out a few positive exhortations in Ecclesiastes does not conclusively demonstrate the purpose or prove the unity of the book. Many interpreters suspect that the text of Ecclesiastes was worked and reworked precisely because, in their view, the positive ethical and spiritual sayings in the book are actually added as counter-balancing rationalizations for what they believe to be the overwhelmingly negative stance of the book as it was originally composed. But the problem with that conjecture is that it is unsupported by any manuscript evidence.

## THE ALLEGED CASE FOR A PLURALITY OF WRITERS

At least three commentators around the beginning of the twentieth century (Carl Siegfried, *Goettinger*

*Handkommentar,* 1898; A. H. McNeile, *An Introduction to Ecclesiastes,* 1904; and George A. Barton, *A Critical and Exegetical Commentary on the Book of Ecclesiastes,* 1908) agreed that corrective additions had been made by two kinds of writers to the basic document originally written under the influence of what they considered to be Greek philosophical thought: a "wisdom writer" (*hakam*) and a "pious interpolator" (*hasid*). In the former category, the three commentators agreed that the following texts should be regarded as additions made by "the wisdom writer": 4:5; 7:11, 12, 19; 8:1; 9:17-18; 10:3, 12-14a, 15. There were many other texts suggested as the work of "the wisdom writer," but on the above list the commentators all concurred. Those texts were isolated proverbs dealing with life and nature, which corrected and enlarged the original document of Ecclesiastes—so it was argued.

There were also those passages attributed to a "pious redactor" (or "pious interpolator"). From the passages suggested, the three scholars agreed on the following list of suspected additions from the pious interpolator's pen: 2:26a; 3:17; 7:29; 8:2b-3a, 5-6a, 11-13; 11:9b; 12:1a. Most commentators who believe Ecclesiastes was reworked include the epilogue of 12:13-14 in this same category of reworked or added texts, although other interpreters attribute it to a fourth writer. Those who believe in the fourth writer think that some religiously inclined Jewish reader of Ecclesiastes "graciously" added some teaching on divine judgment, the divine source of all that exists, and the divine source of all that happens as a mild improvement on an otherwise dreary text.

More recently, some have pointed to a "frame-narrator," because the pronominal references to the "Teacher" in the third-person point to the fact, it is claimed, that the author or editor is someone else. Of course, such third-person so-called frame-narrators (such as are found in 1:1-2; 12:8-10) are known to have existed in the ancient world, but most of the ancient Near Eastern usages serve to name who the author is and under what circumstances he wrote, as for example in a colophon (a note at the end of a book or manuscript). But some want to introduce a third level of identity for a frame-narrator, viz., the first-person recollections and meditations (1:12-14, 16-17; 2:1-13, 14b-26; 3:9-14; 3:16–4:4, 7-8; 5:13-14; 5:16–6:6; 7:15-18, 23-29; 8:9-10; 8:14–9:1; 10:5-7).

However, all three (or four) levels are seamlessly linked together in the book of Ecclesiastes and are mixed in the text without any signs of intrusiveness, often being juxtaposed in the flow of the text. What is more, they all flow together so that we hear one voice, the voice of the author. Duane Garrett has concluded:

> ...there is no reason to suppose that the author who writes "the Teacher says" (the frame-narrator) and the author who gives us the bulk of the book (the Teacher [Qoheleth]) are two different people... When he says, "I, the Teacher" (1:12), any notion that the Teacher and the frame-narrator (or "author/editor") are actually two separate individuals must be abandoned as a fancy of biblical criticism.[4]

Whether Ecclesiastes is the work of more than one writer is, of course, exactly the point that needs to be debated. What is the evidence for multiple authorship of the text? None of our present Hebrew textual traditions suggests any division of labor; instead, the unity of the document

---

4   Duane A. Garrett. *Proverbs, Ecclesiastes, Song of Songs. The New American Commentary* (Nashville, TN: Broadman Press, 1993), vol. 14, pp. 263-4.

is everywhere attested by all Hebrew manuscripts, and the absence of any good reason to suppose that the change in personal pronouns is convincing evidence, in and of itself, for multiple authorship.

How then shall the matter of the purpose and message of this book be settled? Must the result be left to each reader's own preference and subjectivity, with some finding that Ecclesiastes teaches only pessimism, gloom, and doubt, while others extract a message of cheerful industry and the enjoyment of life as a gift from God?

Martin Luther was more than justified in his assessment of the various commentaries on Ecclesiastes. He wrote:

> This book is…one which no one has ever completely mastered. Indeed, it has been so distorted by the miserable commentaries of many writers that it is almost a bigger job to purify and defend the author from the notions which they have smuggled into him than it is to show his real meaning.[5]

## THE AUTHOR'S PURPOSE, PLAN AND SCOPE
## FOR WRITING HIS BOOK

A proper perspective on any book demands that we first come to terms with the author's own intention or stated purpose in writing his book—formerly known as "originalism," or "authorial intention." We must be able to state the author's purpose, plan, and scope. There are three places to which we can go to obtain that sort of information. We can read the preface or introduction to a book, or we can flip quickly to the concluding chapter, especially if it is a mystery, and we wish to

---

5    Martin Luther. *Notes on Ecclesiastes,* 1532, in *Luther's Works* (St. Louis: Concordia Publishing, 1972), vol. 15, p. 7.

know "who done it." A third avenue of pursuit is to skim the contents of the work to identify any repeated refrains, or special hobby horses, that are constant repetitions and emphases in the work. Each of these will be looked at in some detail.[6]

Probably nothing has affected the interpretation of this book more than the statement in its prologue: "*hebel hebelim*," says the Teacher, *hebel hebelim*, everything is *hebel*." If that statement is mistranslated, then chances are that the message of the whole book will be drastically affected as well. In order to get at the best translation of this statement in the prologue, let us look at the epilogue first in order to see what conclusion the author reached in the end.

## THE AUTHOR'S EPILOGUE

Accordingly, let us set aside the prologue of Ecclesiastes for the moment, since it contains one of the most difficult sets of phrases in the book. The epilogue in 12:8-14 *is* probably the most significant clue about what the book is attempting to do. The inattentive and superficial reader might mistake this colophon for what some regard as a pious addition to rescue what appeared to be an otherwise unworthy book for inclusion in the canon of Scripture. Such a conclusion would only add to the impression that Ecclesiastes is a book without any coherence or orderly design.

But once the epilogue is accepted as an original part of the book, that argument evaporates, especially since all of the Hebrew manuscripts we possess of this book include the epilogue of 12:8-14.

Since all too many commentators doubt that the author of the epilogue is the same person who wrote the body of

---

6    This approach was nicely laid out by J. Stafford Wright, "The Interpretation of Ecclesiastes," *Evangelical Quarterly* 18 (1946): pp. 18-34.

Ecclesiastes, it must be demonstrated that there is an intimate connection between the vocabulary and basic ideology of the main body and the epilogue. Among the more prominent links is the theme of 12:14, for example, which claims that there is an appointed time when God will execute His justice over all that is done on earth; but this theme also appears in 11:9; 3:17; and 9:1 as well.

> For God will bring every act into judgment, including every hidden thing, whether good or evil. (12:14)

> ... but know that for all these things God will bring you into judgment. (11:9)

The same promise is given elsewhere in the book.

> I said in my heart, God will judge righteousness and wickedness, for there is a time for every matter and for every work. (3:17)

> I concluded that what the righteous and the wise do are in the hands of God (9:1; cf. 5:8; 12:7).

Another common theme between the epilogue and the body of the book is the command to "fear God" (*Elohim*) found in 12:13. This conclusion to the book is intimately linked with the same command in 3:14; 5:7; 7:18; and 8:12-13 (three times).

> … God does it [i.e., he has placed eternity in the hearts of mortals] so that people will fear him. (3:14)

> Much dreaming and many words are meaningless. Therefore stand in the fear of God. (5:7)

> The person who fears God will avoid all extremes. (7:18)

> I know that it will go better with God-fearing persons who are reverent/fear before God. Yet because the wicked do not fear God, it will not go well with them... (8:12-13)

We must conclude then that these two great themes, (1) *fearing God* and the fact that there is (2) an appointed time for *divine judgment*, were not innovative features lately introduced in the last two verses of the book. Resisting this evidence leads to consistently stripping the rest of the book of most, if not all, spiritual and ethical affirmations. Such radical literary surgery exposes itself to the charge of being subjective and somewhat prejudicial in its canon of literary criticism, for it cares for the problems some believe they see in the text by ruling them out of order on internal and definitional grounds—an unfair way of objectively proceeding. The text must be assumed to be innocent until the evidence proves it to be guilty.

If, as I have argued, a fair case can be made for the unity and integral connection of the epilogue to the rest of the book, then Ecclesiastes does have a deliberate and consciously pursued summary: "The conclusion [Hebrew *soph*, "end"] to the matter" (12:13a) is developed throughout the book. There is a cohesiveness to the "whole thing" (*hakkol dabar*), and the author proceeds to give the theme and purpose of his whole book. Surprisingly enough, it is not "All is vanity," nor is it that everything is just plain "meaningless," as some (e.g., the NIV) are wont to translate the expression; instead, the key to life is to "fear God and keep his commandments," for that is "the entirety" (*hakkol*) of one's being and personality (i.e., the "man-ishness" of a man and "womanly-ness" of a woman) according to this single injunction.

Furthermore, the epilogue asserts that the substance of Ecclesiastes came from the pen of one who was "wise" (*hakam,* 12:9). What he wrote was nothing less than "words of truth" (12:10), "written in uprightness" (12:10) and couched in "pleasant words," or "words of delight" (12:10).

Surely the author's estimate of his own labors, in which "he taught the people knowledge, weighed and studied proverbs with great care" (12:9), hardly gives credence to those who accuse him of being guilty of reasoning after the manner of a natural man immersed in pessimism, skepticism, materialism, fatalism, and the like. He expressed what he did with great care—according to his own estimate of his work!

Nor was the work of the author of Ecclesiastes the result of mere personal experience and experimentalism alone, for the "sayings of the wise," in which category he placed his own work in 12:9, were "given by one Shepherd" (12:11)—a claim that he was divinely aided in writing his book. It hardly seems possible to equate this reference to "one Shepherd" with anyone other than the Lord Himself, who is Yahweh, the one true Shepherd of Israel. That title for our Lord is found in almost every period of Israel's long history in Scripture (Gen. 48:15; 49:24; Ps. 23:1; Isa. 40:11; Jer. 31:10; Ezek. 34:11-12).[7] Therefore, Ecclesiastes has its source in divine revelation just as surely as any other book of the Bible does which likewise claims to be the result of "thus says the Lord." The claim to divine inspiration could not be plainer, or more boldly stated. Ecclesiastes came by revelation from the Lord and was not merely the collection of ordinary human experiences or the like.

As for the Preface, we will suggest what is a better rendering for the Hebrew *hebel*: "transitoriness," or just plain "temporary." The first one to get this right was probably Daniel C. Fredericks in his book *Coping with Transience: Ecclesiastes on the Brevity in Life*. Another who followed in his footsteps was Glenn Fobert, a Canadian layperson who

---

7    Herbert C. Leupold, *Exposition of Ecclesiastes* (Columbus, OH: Wartburg, 1952), p. 295.

wrote a book entitled *Everything Is Mist: Ecclesiastes on Life in a Puzzling and Troubled Temporary World*. More will be said on this in the commentary.

## THE AUTHOR'S CENTRAL THEME
## OR FOCAL POINT

Even among those who admit that Ecclesiastes has a single theme, there are wide differences of opinion over just what that theme is, because so many commentators put an undue emphasis on one or another part of the book, or class of passages in it. For example, Jerome used the book to teach the young woman from Rome, Blessila, the vanity of this present world and that she should choose instead a life of monasticism—all of this in spite of Qoheleth's advice to eat, drink, and enjoy life as a gift from God!

Conversely, others have focused solely on this last piece of advice found in the epilogue, concluding that worldly pleasure is a legitimate good in the plan of God. Now, Ecclesiastes cannot teach that both monasticism and worldly pleasure at one and the same time are both good, desirable outcomes in this life, unless the author was hopelessly involved in a string of self-contradictions and conundrums.

Offering a third view of the theme of Ecclesiastes, others have incorrectly drawn on theories of fatalism and random chance happenings—by attaching an undue prominence and incorrect understanding to such passages as 1:4-11; 3:1-15; 7:13-14; and 9:11, where the fixed order of things in the universe is linked with the definite plan and sovereign will of God. But Qoheleth never denied the freedom of man and thereby argued for confusion and disorder; nor did he suggest that there was a plan of God over all things (wherein nothing was affected by the freedom of mortals) as the overriding theme of his book.

Qoheleth was working on the problem of man's attempt to find meaning in all aspects of God's good world, presumably without coming to know the world's Creator, Sustainer, and Final Judge. For central to all of man's concerns is this problem of integrating life and truth.

That is the issue that appears to have come to a head in 3:11

> God has made everything beautiful in its time; he has also put eternity [*ha'olam*] into man's heart so that he cannot find out what God has done from beginning to the end.

And there the issue hangs. Man has a capacity and desire to know how all things and ideas fit together—the end from the beginning—and yet he cannot know it until he comes to know the One who built men and women in His own image with the capacity to understand who a person is, what that individual means, and what is the worth and meaning of things, events, and life itself. Life, in and of itself, even in God's good world with all its good, God-given gifts, is unable to deliver meaning and joy when it is appropriated in a piecemeal fashion and apart from knowing and believing in God. This, as will be argued later on, and as already noted, is the meaning of the prologue: "Transitoriness of transitoriness, change (or even: "temporality") is everywhere" or "puzzle of puzzles, all is puzzling": namely, that no single part of God's good world can *by itself* unlock the meaning to life. Life, *in and of itself*, is unable to supply the key to the questions of identity, meaning, purpose, value, enjoyment, and destiny. Only in coming to know God can one begin to find answers to these questions.

Especially difficult in trying to understand the meaning of life is the problem of the apparent inequities of divine providence. How can the justice of God be reconciled with the seemingly unmitigated prosperity of the wicked (7:14-15)? Nevertheless, man's entire welfare, even in this area, continues to depend on one thing: whether that person fears God and keeps His commandments, for God will bring every work into judgment—both good and evil. Therefore, all present appearances to the contrary will not be properly understood if this kind of accounting is excluded.

## THE AUTHOR'S REFRAINS

That the analysis just announced is the one set forth by the author of Ecclesiastes can also be demonstrated from a set of refrains that recurs throughout the entire argument. Usually such repetitions underscore what an author is trying to emphasize. For example, the author of Ecclesiastes repeats the following refrain six times: "Eat and drink and make your soul enjoy the good of its labor, for it is a gift of God" (2:24; 3:12-13; 3:22; 5:18-19; 8:15; 9:7-9). That this is not an Epicurean sentiment, as some have argued, is clear, for unlike the Epicureans, Solomon did not end these refrains with "for tomorrow we die," as did the Epicureans.

However, some would discourage us from the objective of laying out the scope and plan of the book by contending that the writer had no such joyful goal in mind. Even the conservative Franz Delitzsch agreed with this negative judgment:

> A gradual development, a progressive demonstration, is wanting, and even the grouping together of the parts is not fully carried out; the connection of thoughts... is external and accidental.... All attempts to show, in the whole, not only oneness of spirit, but a generic progress,

an all-embracing plan, and an organic connection have hitherto failed, and must fail.[8]

Likewise the conservative E. W. Hengstenberg also surprisingly concluded:

> A connected and orderly argument, an elaborate arrangement of parts, is as little to be looked for here as in the special portion of the Book of Proverbs which begins with Chapter X, or as in the alphabetical Psalms.[9]

It is, of course, conceivable that the writer discussed his theme without any orderly arrangement or methodological outline of its various parts. He *may have* just jotted down thoughts as they came to him rather spontaneously, or as one idea provoked an associated concept, all without any logical sequence.

On the other hand, he did come to a "summary" and a "conclusion," or an "end," to his whole work in 12:13-14. Furthermore, he signaled the links in the progress of his thought through the repeated refrain which we have already noted. Thus we must conclude that it is unlikely that he had no plan or outline in mind as he set forth his work. His own words indicate otherwise. In 12:9 he claimed that "he set in order many proverbs," which hardly sounds like a random disarray or jumble of ideas.

## THE AUTHOR'S PROLOGUE

The noun *hebel* occurs sixty-nine times in the Old Testament, five of which refer to the name Abel, the brother Cain killed. Ecclesiastes has thirty-seven or thirty-eight of these

---

8    Franz Delitzsch, *Commentary on the Song of Songs and Ecclesiastes*, trans. M. G. Easton (1877; reprinted in *Commentary on the Old Testament*, C. F. Keil and Franz Delitzsch, Grand Rapids: Eerdmans, 1950), p. 188.

9    Ernst W. Hengstenberg, *Commentary on Ecclesiastes*, trans. D. W. Simon (Philadelphia: Smith, English, & Co., 1860), p. 15.

references (depending on which textual variant is correct in one verse). Some prefer thirty-seven, for that is the numerical value of the Hebrew *hebel* [*hbl*, 5+2+30=37]. Clearly, this word punctuates this book as few other terms do.

Given such a high degree of visibility for this one term, one would expect more agreement among translators and interpreters. "Vanity of vanities" is certainly wrong, for what would that mean? All things are "proud," or they are "stuck up?"[10] The NIV is even more "meaningless" as it rendered it "Meaningless, Meaningless," says the Teacher, "Utterly meaningless!" But if that were so, then why go on reading the book? It was all meaningless anyway!

Later we will make the case that in Ecclesiastes 1:2, the word *hebel* has the sense of "breath, vapor, mist"[11] or the like and thus should be rendered "temporality" or "transition of transitions, everything is changing!" or "change is everywhere!"

## THE AUTHOR'S LOGIC AND THE
## PRESERVATION OF HIS TEXT

Some commentators will grant that the author had a general plan in mind as he wrote, but they say that he also indulged in a number of digressions that are really incidental to his main argument. Alternatively, they propose that the original plan was frustrated by a poor transcription and a general disarrangement of the original sequence of the text through the work of some copyist of the Biblical text.

---

10   W. Sibley Towner. "The Book of Ecclesiastes," in *The New Interpreter's Bible*. (Nashville, TN: Abingdon Press, 1997), vol. V, p. 279.

11   The best critique of the various renderings of *hebel* was done by Glenn Fobert. *Everything Is Mist: Ecclesiastes on Life in a Puzzling and Troubled Temporary World* (Belleville, Ontario: Guardian Books, 2003).

Again, however, without evidence from extant Hebrew manuscripts, the suppositions are groundless. There is no reason to allege such textual corruption or transpositions of sections in the present text. As for the alleged digressions, which apparently would play no part in the central theme of the book, the claim of their existence may be answered best by showing that there is nevertheless a clear plan to the whole book as it stands.

In an unsigned article in *The Princeton Review,* a writer convincingly argued:

> There is a clear and consistent plan in the book of Ecclesiastes, which needs no changes or mutilations...to [expedite] its discovery; one, in fact, of the most strictly logical and methodical kind. Not only is the argument well conducted, conclusive and complete but its various points are so admirably disposed, its divisions so regular, and its different parts so conformed in structure, as to give evidence that the whole was carefully considered and well digested before it was put together. This differs perhaps from the prevalent opinion, but we are convinced that they who complain of a want of method, *haerent in cortice*.[12]

## THE AUTHOR'S OUTLINE

There has been an almost infinite number of schemes suggested for discerning the outline of Ecclesiastes. Without citing all the scholarly apparatus, we can summarize the key divisions among the scholars to be between those who argue for *two* sections (of equal parts: six chapters each; or unequal parts: the first four chapters and the last eight) and those who

---

12 "The Scope and Plan of the Book of Ecclesiastes," *The Princeton Review* 29 (1857): 427. The Latin phrase means "are stuck in the mud."

find *three* sections (of four chapters each)—or even, as we will argue here, *four* divisions of unequal length (chs. 1–2; 3–5; 6–8:15; 8:16–12:14).

The twofold division is usually based on the principle that the first part of Ecclesiastes contains the *theoretical* portion and the second the *practical* portion. Therefore, according to this division, the so-called "vanity" of all earthly things is established in part one, and then part two points out what duties and obligations such truth should elicit from mankind.

It is true that the book becomes more practical and filled with exhortation toward the end of its message, but the separation between doctrine and practice is not that sharp in the book. Notice that practical applications are being made already as early as 2:24-26; 3:10-15, 17, 22; and 5:1-7, 18-20.

Ferdinand Hitzig's suggestion that there are three parts is an attempt to mediate between the twofold and fourfold divisions (*The Preacher Solomon Explained,* 1847). But his suggestion must be rejected because it awkwardly breaks the text, clumsily drawing divisions that override the stylistic hints and rhetorical dividers in the repeated colophons to the sections and the unity of arguments set forth by the writer of Ecclesiastes.

The most satisfactory division of Ecclesiastes, in our view, is one that separates the text into four parts. I was deeply impressed with the breakdown of Ecclesiastes in the previously mentioned article in the *Princeton Review,* which in turn follows Vaihinger's *Studien und Kritiken* (1848), and which Keil had also used in his *Introduction* (1849). This division of Ecclesiastes is as follows:

Part I. 1:2–2:26

II. 3:1–5:20

III. 6:1–8:15

IV. 8:16–12:14

The most obvious advantage of the above fourfold division is that each of the first three sections climaxes with a formal refrain that is given in almost identical terms: "To eat and drink and to realize the benefit of one's labor" is all a gift from God (2:24; 5:18; 8:15).

In 1849, J. G. Vaihinger had argued:

> The design of the Preacher is to propound the immortality of the soul, wherein alone the solution of the otherwise inexplicable problems of life are happily to be found; and to encourage us to look forward to a future judgment, amid the discrepancies between the moral nature and fate of man.[13]

The way Vaihinger analyzed the development of this theme was to view the book as four interwoven poetico-dialectic discourses, all focusing upon the same theme, viz., the vanity of human life, as well as the object and aim of it. Each discourse consists of three parts, which are again subdivided into strophes and half strophes.

DISCOURSE I (chs. i.2–ii.26) shows that by the eternal, unalterably fixed course of all earthly things and the experience of the vain and unsatisfactory strivings after earthly wisdom and selfish gratifications, a God-fearing enjoyment of life, and accepting gratefully the present good, can alone constitute the end of our earthly existence.

---

13   J. G. Vaihinger in Christian D. Ginsburg, *Coheleth: Commonly Called the Book of Ecclesiastes* [1861; reprinted in *The Song of Songs and Coheleth (Commonly Called the Book of Ecclesiastes)*, The Library of Biblical Studies, edited by Harry M. Orlinsky (New York: Ktav, 1970), p. 221.

DISCOURSE II (chs. iii.1–v.19) shows that all our efforts in the world depend upon time and circumstances, and that the success of human labor is altogether controlled by circumstances; the cheerful enjoyment of life, connected with the fear of God and humility, is to be recommended as the highest good.

DISCOURSE III (chs. vi.1–viii.15) shows by the observation that man is frequently deprived of the enjoyment of riches acquired through the favor of God, either from the fault of others or his own, we must try in a nobler way to procure the real and cheerful enjoyment of life, by joyfully using earthly blessings, following higher wisdom, and avoiding folly.

DISCOURSE IV (chs. viii.16–xii.8), considering the melancholy experience of mortals about the inscrutable government of God in the distribution of human destinies, nothing remains to us, besides the exercise of wisdom and the fear of God, for the quieting of our minds. In looking forward to a retributive eternity, and to an otherwise cheerless old age, we are encouraged to enjoy the good and the beautiful in life, especially in our youth and in the vigor of our manhood.[14]

Vaihinger handicapped what in many ways was an excellent treatise with his predilection for finding strophes of equal length. That penchant caused him at times to lose the real argument of the book and develop an artificial thought pattern at several critical points. His overriding concern for mechanical regularity of strophes cost him a proper understanding of the internal arrangements of the thought, even though he divided the sections properly.

---

14   Ibid., pp. 221-2.

The unsigned article in the 1857 *Princeton Review* immeasurably improved on Vaihinger's arrangement of the argument of Ecclesiastes. There was agreement with Vaihinger on the fourfold division of the book. But the argument proceeded in this fashion:

(Chs. i.2–ii.26) A preliminary argument from Solomon's own experience designed to show that happiness is not in man's own power; that all striving and toiling, though it may surround him with every gratification his heart can desire, is powerless to give that gratification itself.

(Chs. iii.1–v.20). [God] has a scheme in which every event and all the multifarious actions of men, with the time of their occurrence, are definitely arranged. This scheme [3:11] is a beautiful one, though from their prevailing worldliness men do not comprehend it.... He [the writer] next proceeds to allege various facts...[or] anomali[es which]...seem to be *so* serious an exception to his grand doctrine that justice rules in the world and happiness attends right-doing...[that] he first utters a caution against being seduced to irreligion, to [the] neglect of religious duty, or to inconsiderate language reflecting upon God's providence by such contemplations.... These wrongs, which are acknowledged to exist, find redress, therefore, in superior government human and divine.

(Chs. vi.1–viii.15) The next step, and this constitutes the central portion of the whole book, is to apply this [i.e., that enjoyment of the world is a gift of God, bestowed by God and regulated by His grand plan] to the explanation of the inequalities of divine providence. ...Prosperity may not be a good...: And adversity or affliction is not necessarily an evil...A right application of the considerations...will remove a large proportion of the apparent inequalities of providence.

(Chs. viii.16–xii.14) The fourth section...is occupied with the removal of discouragements and the enforcing of practical lessons.... The remaining mystery of this subject need be no obstacle to human joy...nor to strenuous activity...while in both their joy and their activity men should be mindful of death and judgment.... The conclusion of the entire discussion is stated to be: Fear God and keep His commandments; for this is the whole welfare of man; for God shall bring every work into judgment, with every secret thing, whether it be good or whether it be evil.[15]

## THE WRITER, THE ADDRESSEES, THE TIMES, AND THE CANONICAL STATUS OF HIS WORK

Some attention should be given to the title, author, audience, and circumstances under which Ecclesiastes was written. Also, the matter of canonicity should be discussed. These will follow immediately.

### THE NAME QOHELETH

Seven times the writer gives to himself the name Qoheleth: three times at the beginning (1:1, 2, 12), three times at the end (12:8, 9, 10), and once in the middle (7:27) of the book. Because Qoheleth appears with the article in 12:8, and, especially because it takes the feminine form of the verb in 7:27, it cannot be a proper name of some individual, but instead must be an appellative, that is, a designation of some sort of function. In form, it is an active feminine participle from the Hebrew verb *qahal,* meaning "to call," then "to call together, to assemble," or "to collect."

---

15   "The Scope and Plan of the Book of Ecclesiastes," pp. 428, 431-2, 433-6, 437-8, 440.

For some, the feminine form of Qoheleth indicated that the word was an abstract designation of an office, the designation being transferred to the person holding that official privilege. But although it is true that feminine forms sometimes express abstracts, Ginsburg complains that they are never formed from the active participle.[16] Keil has responded with the difficult examples of Nehemiah 7:57 (*sophereth*, meaning "scribe" or "leather-worker") and Ezra 2:57 (*Pokereth-hazzebayim*, meaning "the gazelle-tender"), which are actually proper names in those two contexts.[17]

Therefore, it seems best to understand "Qoheleth" as describing the act of "gathering" the people together. That definition matches the use of *qahal* in numerous other biblical passages, where it is invariably used for assembling people, especially for spiritual purposes—hence the Greek name of "Ecclesiastes"—though this is much before the creation of the Church, the *ekklesia*. Therefore, other interpretations (such as "sophist, philosopher, preacher, compiler, collector, penitent, old man, exclaiming voice, departed spirit, eclectic," and "academy") are to be rejected in favor of something more like "Convener" or the "Assembler" of the group.

## IDENTITY OF THE WRITER

Who then was the author who gathered the people together to hear the instruction of this book? In 1:12 the writer says, "I, Qoheleth, became king over Israel in Jerusalem," and in 1:1, the book is prefaced with the claim, "The words

---

16  Ginsburg, p. 9.

17  Karl F. Keil, *Manual of Historico-Critical Introduction to the Canonical Scriptures of the Old Testament*, trans. George C. M. Douglas (Edinburgh: T. & T. Clark, 1869-70), vol. 1, p. 513.

of Qoheleth, son of David, king in Jerusalem." Because Solomon was the only immediate son of David who became king over Israel and reigned in Jerusalem, there can be little doubt that he is the one so specified. Yet the conservative Franz Delitzsch said, "If the Book of *Koheleth* were of old Solomonic origin, then there is no history of the Hebrew language."[18] And a more contemporary scholar, Robert Gordis, was just as definite about the whole matter:

> The view that Solomon is the author has been universally abandoned today, with the growth of a truer recognition of the style, vocabulary and world-outlook of Koheleth.[19]

Nevertheless, even C. D. Ginsburg recognized that Solomonic authorship is "fully corroborated by the unequivocal allusions made throughout this book to particular circumstances connected with the life of this great monarch."[20] Ginsburg invited us to compare, for instance:

Ecclesiastes 1:16 with 1 Kings 3:12 (showing Solomon's unrivaled wisdom);

Ecclesiastes 2:4-10 with 1 Kings 10:16-22 (showing Solomon's unsurpassed wealth);

Ecclesiastes 2:4-10 with 1 Kings 9:20-23 (showing Solomon's huge retinue of servants);

Ecclesiastes 2:4-10 with 1 Kings 10:14-29 (showing Solomon's extensive building operations);

Ecclesiastes 7:20 with 1 Kings 8:46 ("There is no man who does not sin");

---

18   Delitzsch, p. 190.

19   Ibid., Robert Gordis, *Koheleth* (New York: Schocken, 1968), p. 5.

20   Ginsburg, p. 244.

Ecclesiastes 7:28 with 1 Kings 11:1-8 (not a God-fearing woman among a thousand); and

Ecclesiastes 12:9 with 1 Kings 4:32 (showing Solomon to be weighing, studying, and arranging proverbs, ESV).

Still the issue is pressed further: perhaps Solomon might be the "personated author," that is, the actor in whose mouth a later writer placed sentiments that suited him, rather than the real author of the book. The absence of explicit claims of Solomonic authorship found in other works (e.g., the Proverbs of Solomon; the Song of Songs, which is Solomon's; or the Psalms of Solomon—Psalms 72 and 127) is thought to be extremely significant, especially since the title is probably introduced to indicate an ideal or representative role. Qoheleth is consistently used instead of a proper name.

But 1:12 becomes for some the most important piece of evidence in arguing against the Solomonic authorship of this book. The sacred writer represents Solomon as saying that in the *past,* "*I was* (or "*have been*") king over Israel in Jerusalem" (emphasis added). The writer used the perfect tense of the verb "to be" (*hayit*). Thus it is said that Solomon either was king and continued to be so or that he was no longer king when this text was composed. Some who oppose Solomonic authorship read the verb "to be" as a past tense "was" and conclude that the actual Solomon had long since passed away as the present author of this book now spoke.

The above argument for the past tense will not bear all the weight it is called to bear. The Hebrew perfect tense actually denotes a state of action that began in the past and stretches forward to the present. Only in later Hebrew is it restricted solely to past events. Nevertheless, this form of the verb would be proper even if Solomon were writing it, for as

George Barton noted, the same form was used by Moses when he named his son Gershom ("sojourner"—I *was*," or better still "*have been* a sojourner" in a foreign land [Exod. 2:22, ESV]) and by the linguistic example of the pleading brothers to an unrecognized Joseph: "We are all sons of one man, we are honest men, your servants *were* not [or "*have not been*"] spies" (Gen. 42:11).[21] So Solomon could be understood to have said: "I have been king"—and I continue to be such to this day!

Thus we see that Hebrew can be deliberately indefinite about the time aspect of a verb, and that was the way the author wanted it in 1:12.

But 1:12 is not the only passage presenting an alleged difficulty to Solomonic authorship. In 1:16, the writer compares himself advantageously "over all who were before me in Jerusalem." Since David was the only Hebrew ruler to precede Solomon *in Jerusalem* in the Davidic line, the words are hardly appropriate in Solomon's mouth—so the argument goes. But Hengstenberg[22] has argued that even if the phrase is limited to kings, the reference is probably to the previous line of Canaanite kings who preceded Solomon in Jerusalem, such as Melchizedek (Gen. 14:18), Adonizedek (Josh. 10:1), and Araunah (2 Sam. 24:23). That easily cares for the issue.

A single argument left in favor of a post, or non-Solomonic origin for Ecclesiastes is the character of its language. On this basis, even such conservative scholars

---

21  George A. Barton, *A Critical and Exegetical Commentary on the Book of Ecclesiastes* (1908; reprinted in *The International Critical Commentary*, edited by Samuel R. Driver, Alfred Plummer, and Charles A. Briggs; Edinburg: T. & T. Clark, 1959), p. 8.

22  Hengstenberg, pp. 60-1.

as Hengstenberg, Delitzsch, Leupold, and E. J. Young felt compelled to date the book in the fifth century B.C., and others placed it in the Greek period from the third century B.C. to the time of Herod the Great.

Here again, however, the linguistic evidence does not support the conclusion reached. There is first of all the matter of the complete absence of any Hebrew consonants used as vowels or helping letters, which absence points to an exceptionally early composition of the book. Final vowel letters (*matres lectionis*) first appeared in the late eighth century B.C. and medial, or middle, vowel letters came into vogue at the end of the seventh or early sixth century B.C., all of which are missing here. [23]

Furthermore, many of the sometimes cited twenty-nine alleged Aramaisms (which normally occur from the fifth century B.C. down to 200 B.C.) are actually of Canaanite-Phoenician vintage, according to Mitchell Dahood,[24] and therefore of much earlier usage. In fact, it is almost impossible to avoid the conviction that Ecclesiastes is of such a unique and special genre that it currently fits into no known period of the history of the Hebrew language. Archer and Dahood both repeat Jastrow's and Margoliouth's judgment that it is impossible to explain the peculiarities of Qoheleth's grammar, syntax, and orthography on the basis that it is late Mishnaic Hebrew or late Aramaic.[25] To support

---

23  Gleason Archer, "The Linguistic Evidence for the Date of Ecclesiastes," *Journal of the Evangelical Theological Society* 12 (1969): 171.

24  Mitchell Dahood, "Canaanite-Phoenician Influence in Qoheleth," *Biblica* 33 (1952): 201-2.

25  Archer, p. 170; Dahood, pp. 30-1; Morris Jastrow, Jr. and David S. Margoliouth, "The Book of Ecclesiastes," in *The Jewish Encyclopedia*, ed. Isidore Singer (New York: Funk and Wagnalls, 1901-6), vol. 5, p. 33.

his judgment, Margoliouth pointed to: (1) the frequency of the participial present forms; (2) the ungarbled nature of certain phrases in later times; (3) the complete omission of the name Yahweh; (4) the failure to allude to anything from previous Hebrew history; and (5) the absence of any of the newer Jewish words for "business," "lest," or "authorize."

But if the internal evidence, with its similarities to the phrases, style of life, and experience of the Davidic King Solomon depicted in 1 Kings 1–11, and the external linguistic evidence suggest that the orthography, lexicography, and even syntax of Ecclesiastes may reach back into the tenth century B.C., i.e., to the days of Solomon, there is no reason why we should not conclude that the writer and speaker of this book was Solomon, son of King David.

The predominant ideas found in Ecclesiastes, namely, wisdom and the fear of God, as well as their application to secular and sacred life, likewise fit the character of Solomon as set forth in 1 Kings 3–5 and the book of Proverbs.

## THE TEXT OF ECCLESIASTES

The present Hebrew Masoretic text appears to be in a good state of preservation. It is supported by the ancient versions of the Greek Septuagint, as well as the Aramaic, Syriac, and Latin versions. Later in the Middle Ages would come Ethiopic and Arabic versions as well. The Septuagint, surprisingly, is a very literal translation of the Hebrew.

Qumran has given to us two fragments of the text of Ecclesiastes: 4QQoha and 4QQohb, which date to somewhere around 175 B.C. (To have copies of the book in Hebrew this early means that the text must have been composed somewhat earlier, an argument that would help our contention that the book is Solomonic, for in previous dates set for Ecclesiastes, the second century B.C. was about the time most wanted to date the book.) These fragments represent the text in Ecclesiastes 1:10-14; 5:14-18; 6:1, 3-8, 12; 7:1-10, 19-20. The only noticeable variants are in the alternate spelling of some of the words. The only variation in the numbering of the Hebrew verses in later versions is that Hebrew 4:17-5:19 equals English 5:1-20.

## THE DATE AND PURPOSE OF ECCLESIASTES

At what stage in Solomon's life did he write Ecclesiastes? And what was his purpose in writing the book? The book may be read as best fitting that period of Solomon's life just after his love for his Lord was stolen by his practice of idolatry and his outrageous violation of the principle of monogamous marriage, but to the contrary, 12:9 appears to say that Solomon wrote Ecclesiastes while he was composing and collecting many proverbs. The former view is preserved, in part, from what the Jewish legend with its Aramaic paraphrase of 1:12 proposed:

> When King Solomon was sitting upon the throne of his kingdom, his heart became greatly elated with riches, and he transgressed the commandment of the Word of God; and he gathered many houses, and chariots, and riders, and he amassed much gold and silver, and he married wives from foreign nations. Whereupon the anger of the Lord was kindled against him, and he sent to him Ashmodai, the king of the demons, and he drove him from the throne of his kingdom, and took away the ring from his hand, in order that he should roam and wander about in the world, to reprove it; and he went about the provincial towns and cities in the land of Israel, weeping and lamenting, and saying, "I am Coheleth, whose name was formerly called Solomon, who was King over Israel in Jerusalem."[26]

---

26  Targum on Ecclesiastes 1:12. See also *The Jerusalem Talmud*, tractate Sanhedrin 20c.

The introduction of Ashmodai, king of the demons, and a period of dethronement are, of course, sub-biblical and call for no further comment. But the connection of Solomon's sinful backsliding with the occasion of the book is at least noteworthy.

Could it be that the picture of old age in 12:1-6 contains the autobiographical mark? Yet even this argument can be turned on its head, for younger men can adequately describe the problems of old age based on their observations of others.

Solomon was given another name from the Lord when he was born—Jedidiah, "Beloved of the Lord" (2 Sam. 12:24-25). Indeed, he was promised personal adoption and mercy as God's own son (2 Sam. 7:14-15). Yet the Lord was angry with his "son" when "his heart had turned away from the Lord, the God of Israel" (1 Kings 11:9). Therefore, the Lord "appeared to him twice" (1 Kings 11:9). Then he "raised up adversar[ies] against him" (1 Kings 11:14, 23) and used them as the rod of affliction to turn Solomon from his backsliding.

Did those measures have any effect? And is our book of Ecclesiastes a witness to any possible effect and a result of those divine evidences of the love of God had on his life? The answer to both questions is "yes." There is in the book an air of repentance and humility for past values and performance. Then there is the matter of later books using both David and Solomon as models for the expected Messianic kingdom (1 and 2 Chron.) or as the "way"; that is, the lifestyles of both David and Solomon were considered to be worthy of emulation (2 Chron. 11:17). The reference to Solomon's "wisdom," even in the "rest of his days," could be a reference to the end of his life (1 Kings 11:41).

The writer of 1 Kings 11:41 assured his readers that the record of the rest of what Solomon "did and his wisdom" was written in "the book of the Acts of Solomon." Although some have wondered out loud if Ecclesiastes might be the book referred to in 1 Kings 11:41, that would appear to be improbable, because no such title as "The Acts of Solomon" has ever been found to be attached to any known manuscript of Ecclesiastes, or any other known manuscript for that matter. Nevertheless, that Solomon did experience repentance and restoration, even as did that Davidite Manasseh (which was a reversal of a half-century of evil and sin), would have gone unnoticed had not a relatively small, later, footnote-like statement about Manasseh been included in 2 Chronicles 33:18-20. Therefore, given the Solomonic authorship of the book, it may be best if it is placed neither *before* his apostasy, for the questions and sins of Ecclesiastes did not seem to trouble him then, nor *during* his years of rebellion, for then he had no occasion to use the language of spiritual things. While Ecclesiastes may be placed *after his* apostasy, when both his recent turmoil and repentance were still fresh in his mind, this cannot be demonstrated and the question must remain open.

Why, then, it may be asked, was Solomon so stingy with his references to Yahweh's previous mercies to Israel? Indeed, the book may be further faulted in that (1) it never used the covenant name of Yahweh, but rather twenty-eight times used Elohim ("God"), a name generally used when there is reference to God's work as Creator and Sustainer for all men apart from any work of grace in salvation; and (2) it may also be faulted because there is no mention of the Mosaic law; nor (3) is there any treatment to any aspect of the special features of God's call or guidance of Israel in her history.

However, even these objections are not without an alternative suggestion. For example, one idea that goes a long way toward answering the "faults" in the paragraph above is that Solomon may have intentionally written Ecclesiastes with an eye to a wider circle of readers than just the Hebrews—perhaps those from the Aramaean and the other Semitic nations that were then subject to his government and those nations that had caused a good deal of his spiritual downfall through his attempt to placate his numerous wives, who hailed from their states. Such a "cosmopolitan tendency" would be most appropriate for wisdom literature, which had the aim of raising a voice to "the sons of men" at large so that all might hear (Prov. 8:4). The book would then have a missionary flavor as it attempted to use a sort of what we now call "cultural apologetics," to call Gentiles (along with those in Israel) at large to straighten out their thinking, acting, values, and preparation for their eternal destiny. The point of contact, especially with those pagans, would be the ancient hope, "O that we might see some good!" (Ps. 4:6), or the questions of Micah 6:6 and Deuteronomy 10:12: "With what shall I come before the Lord?" and "What does the Lord your God require of you?"

Had not the Queen of Sheba in her faraway setting among the Gentiles heard of the famed wisdom of Solomon and his ability to answer difficult questions (1 Kings 10:1)? It may be surmised that requests such as hers provided the reason for making a discussion such as Ecclesiastes available to a wider audience of Gentiles. Thus the fundamental principles, or first steps, in godliness were set forth for those who had the longest spiritual road to travel. A "missionary message" to the Gentiles would have to begin with those issues that affect all men, because all share the image of God and yet are involved in a world that is often unintelligible and hostile.

The call for such a treatise as this was also to be found in the directive given by Moses in Deuteronomy 4:6-8:

> Keep [my statutes and commandments] and do them; for that will be your wisdom and your discernment *in the eyes of the peoples,* who, *when they hear all these statutes, will say,* "What a wise and discerning people is this great nation!" Where is there a great nation that has a god so near to it as the Lord *our* God is whenever we call on him? Where is there a great nation that has statutes and ordinances so fair as this whole law which I am placing before you today? (emphasis added).

Solomon was eminently qualified to set forth wisdom before the "eyes of the peoples" at large, just as he had done in Proverbs. Instead of being transformed by the culture and the times of his subject nations and his Gentile allies, he would begin with the very basic questions of life: What is good? What is worthwhile? What is life meant to accomplish? How can anyone satisfy that gnawing thirst to find out "the end from the beginning" and bridge that "eternity" in the "heart" of all men (3:11)?

On the other hand, the book must not be viewed as being totally out of keeping with the distinctive message found in the divine revelation up to that Solomonic portion of time in the united monarchy, which dates from approximately 1000 to 931 B.C. One of the central points of the book is the key that connects Ecclesiastes to the theology of previous wisdom and Torah texts: "Fear God," for this is what life is all about.

The book of Deuteronomy had made "the fear of the Lord" a focal point of concern (Deut. 4:10; 5:29; 6:2, 13, 24; 8:6; 10:12, 20; 13:4; 14:23; 17:19; 28:58; 31:12-13).

Indeed, "to fear the Lord" was to commit oneself to Yahweh by faith, as did *some* of the Egyptians (Exod. 9:20, 30) who formed part of the "mixed multitude" that left Egypt with Israel (Exod. 12:38). That fear was not some extraordinary, numinous feeling of terror, or even of awe, but instead it was an attitude of receptivity that manifested itself in belief, obedience, and love for the living God. That attitude had already appeared—on Mount Moriah when Abraham willingly offered his son Isaac (Gen. 22:12) and in Joseph's believing response (Gen. 42:18). If Job is to be placed in the patriarchal era, then he, too, must be cited as an early example of what our book of Ecclesiastes is urging (Job 1:1, 8-9; 2:3). Another example is the midwives who evidenced the same attitude of obedient faith (Exod. 1:17, 21). In fact, to "fear God" is to live—and to live more abundantly (Lev. 19:14, 32; 25:17, 36, 43; Prov. 10:27; 14:27; 19:23; 22:4). Such teaching about the "fear of the Lord" is "a fountain of life" (Prov. 13:14; 14:27). Why should any person, created by God in His image, joylessly endure life as a burden, only to finally face the judgment of God as a further blow after having missed their own purpose, joy, and meaning in this life?

The second mark of continuity in Ecclesiastes with previous Scripture is the injunction to "keep His commandments." Failure to do so will not only rob the rebel of his present enjoyment of that list of earthly blessings promised in Leviticus 26 and Deuteronomy 28 to all who would walk in the way of the Lord; but disobedience to God's commandments will also expose the wicked "every day," as well as in that final day, to the anger and judgments of God (Ps. 7:11). The prominence of judgment in the book of Ecclesiastes is seen easily from the following citations:

The righteous and the wicked God will judge. (3:17)

*Why* should God be angry at your voice and destroy the work of your hands? (5:6b)

Although a sinner does evil a hundred times and protracts his life, yet I know it will be well with those fearing God because they fear in His presence. But it will not be well with the wicked, neither will he protract his days like a shadow, because there is no fear in the presence of God. (8:12-13)

But know that for all these things [walking in the ways of your heart] God will bring you into judgment. (11:9b)

The spirit returns to God who gave it. (12:7b)

For God shall bring every work to judgment with every secret deed, whether good or evil. (12:14)

The most startling text is Ecclesiastes 11:9, which some say directly contradicts Numbers 15:39b, which reads: "You shall remember all the commandments of the Lord and obey them and not follow after your own heart and your own eyes, which you are inclined to go after lustily." The men who produced Codex B of the Greek translation of the Old Testament (the Septuagint) reacted so strongly to Ecclesiastes 11:9 that they inserted a "not" in "walk in the ways of your heart." The Jewish *Targums* paraphrase 11:9 similarly.

But was Qoheleth contradicting the Pentateuch in 11:9 by advising young people to enjoy themselves and follow the leading of their hearts and eyes? Scholars who argue that there is a blatant contradiction also argue that the warning following that advice in 11:9 was added later for purposes of orthodoxy: "But know that for all these things God will bring you into judgment."

However, no evidence exists to support the theory that Qoheleth's view contradicted the Pentateuch. Does not the same hand who wrote and taught 11:9 also argue at the end of the book that God will bring every work, every secret deed—much less the leading of your heart and eyes—into judgment to ascertain whether it was good or evil? Consequently, Solomon does not condone a hedonistic Epicureanism, or even a relativistic stance that judges the worth of everything by one's own feelings. He urges enjoyment, but likewise cautions that even that rejoicing is reviewable by the God who judges all.

Finally, in linking Ecclesiastes to Scripture that preceded it, we can refer briefly to those wisdom sayings that Ecclesiastes shares with other Scriptures. For example, "He who digs a pit shall fall into it" (10:8) is also found in Proverbs 26:27. Another reference in Ecclesiastes, "The dust returns to the earth as it was" (3:20; 12:7), carries the same sentiment as Genesis 3:19b: "You are dust, and you will return to the dust" (see also Gen. 2:7). Many other echoes of Genesis 1–11 can be listed as follows:

- Man is to live in companionship (Gen. 1:27; Eccles. 4:9-12; 9:9).

- Man is given to sin (Gen. 3:1-6; Eccles. 7:29; 8:11; 9:3).

- Knowledge has God-given limits (Gen. 2:17; Eccles. 8:7; 10:14).

- Life since the Fall involves tiresome toil (Gen. 3:14-19; Eccles. 1:3; 2:22).

- Death is inevitable for all mankind (Gen. 3:19, 24; Eccles. 9:4-6; 11:8).

- Order and regularity of nature are God's sign of blessing (Gen. 8:21–9:17; Eccles. 3:11-12).

- Life is a "good" gift from God (Gen. 1:10, 12, 18, 21, 25, 31; Eccles. 2:24, 26; 3:12-13; 5:18).

Accordingly, creation theology provides a strong context for the theology of Qoheleth.[27]

Thus we must conclude that Solomon was aware of and was consciously writing in the stream of antecedent theology and revelation as found in the books known to the Jews prior to the monarchy. His "cosmopolitan" and "universal" stance was deliberately taken to: (1) match the special genre he had decided to use as a medium for his work; (2) gain as wide an audience among the Gentiles as possible; and (3) set a new standard of godliness for potential proselytes and Gentiles in general (without abandoning the implications of the same teaching for believing Israelites as well) in a society and culture filled with every form of idolatry, indecency, and injustice known to man.

It should be fairly easy to see why Ecclesiastes was included in the canon of Scripture. There was no doubt that Ecclesiastes, or Qoheleth, was to be included in that canon which the Jews received as inspired (the Mishnah uses the expression that it "pollute[d] the hands," due to its holiness, to indicate its inspiration). And there was no doubt, according to the evidence of the third century B.C. Greek translation, called the Septuagint, and the argument of Josephus, the translations of Aquila, Symmachus, and Theodotion in the first two Christian centuries, and the catalog of Melito, Bishop of Sardis about A.D. 170, that Ecclesiastes belonged to the canon of Old Testament Scripture.

---

27 Charles Forman, "Koheleth's Use of Genesis," *Journal of Semitic Studies* 5 (1960): 254-63; Walter Zimmerli, "The Place and Limit of Wisdom in the Framework of Old Testament Theology," *Scottish Journal of Theology* 17 (1964): 145-58.

The oft-repeated charge that the Talmud and Midrashim were ambivalent about Ecclesiastes' place in the canon is an overstatement and a misunderstanding of the facts of the case. If the charge is that there were some serious questions about how to *interpret* Ecclesiastes, the answer is that the problem was not confined to Qoheleth; the same problems existed with the Song of Solomon, Proverbs, and certain Psalms. Further, those objections were all from the school of Shammai, whose rules of interpretation were hotly contested by the school of Hillel. Shammai was, in fact, overruled by the seventy elders, and so the Synagogue had settled the issue. What is more, the complaint this school raised, viz., that the words of Qoheleth contradict one another, was only an apparent difficulty that was resolved just as alleged internal contradictions of the same kind in Proverbs were resolved: by careful exegesis of the text.

## ALLUSIONS TO ECCLESIASTES IN THE NEW TESTAMENT

There appear to be a number of links between the book of Ecclesiastes and the New Testament. Especially frequent are allusions that are made to the discourses of Jesus. These may be summarized as follows:

| Ecclesiastes 1:1 | with | Luke 13:34 |
|---|---|---|
| Ecclesiastes 2:24 | with | Matt. 11:19 |
| Ecclesiastes 3:1 | with | John 7:30 |
| Ecclesiastes 3:2 | with | John 16:21 |
| Ecclesiastes 4:17[28] | with | Luke 23:34 |
| Ecclesiastes 5:1 | with | James 1:19 |

---

28    In Hebrew, it is Ecclesiastes 4:17, yet in English it is Ecclesiastes 5:1.

| Ecclesiastes 5:1 | with | Matt. 6:7, 8 |
| Ecclesiastes 5:5; 12:6 | with | James 3:6 |
| Ecclesiastes 7:18 | with | Matt. 23:23 |
| Ecclesiastes 9:10 | with | John 9:4 |
| Ecclesiastes 11:5 | with | John 3:8 |

These and other possible allusions in the Pauline literature encourage us to see that Ecclesiastes was not regarded as an orphan book with no connections with other books in the Bible.

## THE COMPARISON OF ECCLESIASTES WITH ANCIENT NEAR EASTERN TEXTS

Some scholars believe that they have found the roots of the sentiments and advice of Qoheleth in the literature of the Near East. Especially striking in the minds of many is a possible parallel between Ecclesiastes 9:7-10 and a section from the "Gilgamesh Epic," tablet X, column III (otherwise known as the "Babylonian Flood Story") from approximately 2000 B.C.).

Gilgamesh, where are you wandering?
You will never find the life you look for.
For when the gods created man,
They let death be his share,
and life they withheld in their own hands.
Gilgamesh, fill your belly—Be merry day and night,
Let your days be full of joy,
Dance and make music day and night.
Let your garments be fresh, wash your head and bathe.
Pay attention to the child holding your hand,
And let your wife delight in your embrace.
These things alone are the task of men[?].
None cometh from thence [i.e., from the place of the dead]

that he may tell us how they fare,
that he may tell us what they need,
that he may set our heart at rest [?],
until we also go to the place whither they are gone.[28]

From the third millennium B.C. came the Egyptian wisdom text called the "Instruction of Ptahhotep," a description of old age, a subject Qoheleth pursued in Ecclesiastes 12:3-7:

Old age hath come and dotage hath descended. The limbs are painful and the state of being old appeareth as something new. Strength hath perished for weariness. The mouth is silent and speaketh not. The eyes are shrunken and the ears deaf.... The heart is forgetful and remembereth not yesterday. The bone, it suffereth in old age, and the nose is stopped up and breatheth not. To stand up and to sit down are alike ill. Good is become evil. Every taste hath perished.[29]

In the first selection from the "Gilgamesh Epic," the young woman, Siduri, the winemaker, gives Gilgamesh advice on the goal of life. But in Ecclesiastes 9:7-10 there is no resignation, as there is in Siduri's advice. Instead, Solomon says, "Go on, eat, enjoy your food, and drink your wine with a happy heart, since already God has approved your deed." However, Solomon does not embrace hedonism. Life, whether it be play or work, is subject to current and final reviews by God. Siduri wrongly believed that mankind should only play and that life after death was withheld from all persons; but that

---

29 Author's paraphrase. A translation can be found in H. Frankfort et al., *Before Philosophy* (Harmondsworth, UK: Pelican, 1949), p. 226.

30 Adolf Erman, *The Literature of the Ancient Egyptians*, trans. Aylward M. Blackman (1927; reprinted as *The Ancient Egyptians: A Sourcebook of Their Writings*, New York: Harper & Row, 1966), p. 55.

is hardly the message of Ecclesiastes. Such a morbid prospect can be found elsewhere—for example, in the Egyptian funeral banquet song known as "The Song of the Harpist":

> Be glad.... Follow thy desire, so long as thou livest.
> Put myrrh on thine head, clothe thee in fine linen,
> and anoint thee.... and vex not thine heart,—
> until that day of lamentation cometh to thee.[30]

In this piece (which is alleged to reflect the sentiments of Eccles. 2:24; 3:12-13; 5:17; 9:7-9; and 11:7-9), the friends of the deceased gathered in the tomb and, surrounded by flowers, wine, a meal, and music, heard this section along with Siduri's theme of the enjoyment of life. Solomon's list is in the form of an allegory and focuses on a somewhat different set of geriatric signs.

The "Instruction of Ptahhotep," quoted above on old age, is fair enough and has some vague similarities to Ecclesiastes 12:3-7. But the "Instruction of Ptahhotep" has another word of advice that is said to be similar to Ecclesiastes 5:18-19: "Every man also to whom God has given wealth." That word of advice reads:

> Reverence [the man of repute] in accordance with what hath happened unto him, for wealth cometh not of itself....
> It is God that createth repute.... The vestibule [of the great] hath its rule...It is God who assigneth the foremost place.[31]

Obviously, on the basis of these samples, it is clear that Solomon did not borrow any of his materials for Ecclesiastes *en bloc* from the Egyptians, even though they perhaps may supply the best parallels from the Near East

31   Erman, p. 133.

32   Ibid., pp. 58-9.

to his book. Neither was he party to their pessimistic views about death.

Surprisingly, Solomon and the Egyptian writers did, however, share many common topics. The light of the doctrine of "common grace" is evident, especially in the last citation from the "Instruction of Ptahhotep," where one's position of eminence in government and wealth both came from God alone. Moreover, from the earliest times, the search for the worth, meaning, and goal of life was such a burning issue in the hearts of men that Solomon properly addressed himself to this wider audience of readers on the very perplexity that threatened their existence. But in no way was the final shape of our canonical book of Ecclesiastes affected, as any fair reading of this evidence will demonstrate. The similarities are that they all shared a joy for living life and a concern about old age—its disenablements—and its regard for wisdom. Solomon was undoubtedly aware of this Egyptian literature, but, as 1 Kings 4:29-32 says, he excelled "all the people of the East and all the wisdom of Egypt"— and that had to be a remarkable feat attributable only to the gift of God. It may also be observed that if Solomon was addressing the larger Gentile audience in this book, then he deliberately introduced those themes and sayings that could have easily "built bridges" with them as well.

## THE OCCASION FOR READING ECCLESIASTES IN LATER TIMES

One final remark might help to set the tone for us. Ecclesiastes was intended to be a book in celebration of "joy" and of God's "good" creation. In Judaism, this book was read on the third day of the Feast of Tabernacles. It is most unlikely, as

O.S. Rankin suggested,[32] that this reading was done to bring some sobering thoughts about the brevity and seriousness of life into the midst of all the levity and cheerfulness of that festival. Had not Nehemiah rebuked the people of his day for mixing weeping and mourning with the Feast of Tabernacles (Neh. 8:9)? His advice was that they should:

> Go on, eat the rich food and drink sweet wine
> and send gifts to those who cannot provide for themselves,
> for this day is holy to our Lord;
> and do not be sad,
> for the joy of the Lord is your strength. (Neh. 8:10)

Constantly, Solomon likewise advocated joy and rejoicing, because life is a gift from God. Very few commentators have featured this emphasis on *simchah* ("joy") in Ecclesiastes; among the few who have are: Robert Gordis, Edwin Good, Nobert Lohfink, and Robert Johnston.[33] In fact, this Hebrew root *simchah,* meaning "joy, gladness, enjoyment," along with the verb *samach,* meaning "to be glad," "to rejoice in," appears seventeen times in Ecclesiastes. Johnston pointed out that in the Old Testament, *samach* may refer to communal jubilation for a festival, a gathering for religious ritual purposes (see Ps. 45:15), or the individual mood of joy (see Prov. 14:13).

So, the mood of Ecclesiastes is one of delight, with the prospect of living and enjoying all the goods of life once man has come to fear God and keep His commandments.

---

33   O.S. Rankin in *The Interpreter's Bible,* ed. George A. Buttrick, 12 vols. (Nashville: Abingdon, 1951-7), 5:4.

34   Gordis, p. 131; Edwin Good, *Irony in the Old Testament* (Philadelphia: Westminster Press, 1965), p. 191; Norbert Lohfink, *The Christian Meaning of the Old Testament* (London: Burns & Oates, 1969), pp. 154-5; and Robert Johnston, "'Confessions of a Workaholic': A Reappraisal of Qoheleth," *Catholic Biblical Quarterly* 38 (1976): 17-28.

# 1

# ENJOYING LIFE AS A GIFT FROM GOD

## Ecclesiastes 1:1–2:26

Unlike the stories of the Old Testament, Ecclesiastes is not a narrative with a plot line running through it, exhibiting an easily identifiable beginning, a climactic high point somewhere in the middle, and an ending. Nevertheless, there is a strong progression of thought found within this book, despite strong declamations by a host of commentators to the contrary. What unifies this book is the assertion that there is a *God-given joy* that can be found in life even though a strong bass-pedal note of "breath," "mist," "transience" or "change" is played against the more central search for some kind of fixed point of reference and meaning in one's work. This book points to learning and living, that yields enjoyment to life itself and joy in such basic functions of life such as eating, drinking and happiness in one's work.

### THE MEANING OF HEBREW *HEBEL*
This bass-pedal note, to speak metaphorically for the moment, is struck immediately in Ecclesiastes 1:2 with its fivefold repetition of the Hebrew word *hebel*: "*hebel hebalim*, says the Teacher, *hebel hebalim*, everything is *hebel*"—traditionally

rendered, "Vanity of vanities," says the Teacher, "vanity of vanities! All is vanity."

But is that the correct meaning of *hebel*? What has traditionally been rendered as "vanity," "emptiness" or "meaninglessness," is literally "breath, vapor, mist, smoke."[1] It would appear, argued layman Fobert in his excellent study, that the assumption for most commentators was that "vapor, breath" and similar renderings of *hebel* implied "emptiness, futility, vanity, or meaninglessness." But was that a fair way to render *hebel*?

These negative translations seem to have begun with the improper rendering that the Septuagint (completed around 280 B.C.) gave to this key term. In that Greek translation of the Bible, *hebel* was rendered by the Greek word *mataiotes* (the Greek word used in Romans 8:20), which does mean "emptiness," "futility" or "purposelessness." Jerome (c. A.D. 345–c. 419) more or less sealed this tradition when he rendered *hebel* in the Latin Vulgate as "*vanitas*," which the King James followed with its "vanity" and the NIV furthered with its adjectival rendering of the Hebrew noun *hebel* as "meaningless."

But not all the early translations followed the lead of the Septuagint, for Aquila (A.D. 117-138), Theodotion (second-century A.D.) and Symmachus (late second-century A.D.) used a different Greek term, namely: *atmos*, or *atmis*, "breath" or "mist." Moreover, a number of modern translations rendered *hebel* in a concrete (as opposed to an abstract or metaphorical) manner in other Old Testament books—"vapor, breath, fog." On other occasions, the shortness, or the brevity, of life was found in the root idea of this word, as for example

---

1    Glenn Fobert, *Everything Is Mist: Ecclesiastes on Life in a Puzzling and Troubled Temporary World* (Belleville, Ontario: Guardian Books, 2003), pp. 31-6.

in Psalm 39:5, 6, 11 ("Each person's life is but a breath... Each one is but a breath", NIV). It could be said, of course, that "breath" is invisible; therefore, it too can be associated metaphorically with "nothingness" and "emptiness." "Mist," on the other hand, can be seen, like a "fog." But so could "breath" be seen on a cold day.

In a strikingly similar manner, the book of James in the New Testament (4:13-15) likens a person's life to "the morning fog—it's here for a while and then it's gone." The Greek word that James used here is related to the Greek form preferred by Aquila, Theodotion and Symmachus: *atmis*. Therefore, James used the concrete form of this word to signify that the mist or fog was "temporary" and "transient." Could it be that James had Ecclesiastes in mind when he used this term? Surely, James was not cynical about life, or one who had despaired of living, as some accuse Qoheleth of being. James, then, appears to have rejected *mataiotes*, with its meaning of "emptiness" or the like, in preference for *atmis*, "mist" or "fog," which emphasized the "*transience*" and "*changes*" that come in life instead. There is also another aspect of "mist" or "fog," and that is that in addition to being temporary, it makes things difficult to discern and therefore probably carries the idea of being "puzzling" as well. So with this as a fresh starting point, let us see the difference this new rendering of the introduction to this book makes to the commentary on the whole book.

## VIEWING THE CALL FOR US TO ENJOY LIFE FROM THE CONCLUSION OF THE SECTION: ECCLESIASTES 2:24-26

The writer of Ecclesiastes believed that his book was an argument that came to a grand conclusion in 12:13-14.

Therefore, we can fairly propose, as was argued in the introductory chapter, that each of his four sections added something to the progress and development of that argument. Consequently, the best way to begin to analyze the book is to look at each of the four *conclusions* to the four sections of the book, which in the first section comes in Ecclesiastes 2:24-26. By this means, we should be able to determine where the writer, Solomon, believed the first section of his argument led him in its argumentation. If we can accurately understand that sub-conclusion, we might then be able to follow with greater certainty the approach he took in leading up to that first step toward the grand conclusion to his whole book.

The first section of Ecclesiastes ends by saying:

²⁴There is nothing [inherently] good in a person [to enable one] to eat, drink and cause one's soul to see good in one's labor. Even this, I myself realized, was from the hand of God.

²⁵For apart from him [God], who can eat and who can find enjoyment?

²⁶For to the person who is pleasing before him, he [God] gives wisdom, knowledge and joy; but to the sinner he gives the task of gathering and amassing [things or wealth?], [only] to give to one who is pleasing in God's sight. This too is a puzzle/transitory and a vexation of spirit.

Two principles are quickly established from these verses:

- The *possession* of the blessings and "goods" of life are a gift from God. All good things must be received and understood as coming from the hand of God if they are to be used properly and joyfully.

- Men and women definitely do not have it within themselves or in their own innate *abilities* to extract enjoyment from life or from any of life's most mundane functions, such as eating, drinking, or enjoying the purchasing power of a paycheck. Only God can give that ability to those who come to Him in belief, even for such basic functions of life, not to mention even higher values.

This translation of 2:24-26, and the two principles derived from it, must, of course, be substantiated by the passage itself. Especially noticeable is the fact that we did *not* translate verse 24 to say, "There is nothing *better than*…," or "A man can do nothing *better than*…"; however, a somewhat similar phrase indicating such a comparison does appear later on, for example, in 3:12 and 8:15. Scholars uniformly assume that a Hebrew word indicating "than" (Hebrew *min,* "from") has dropped out of the Hebrew text of 2:24, because it does appear in the other two passages. But no textual evidence supports that assumption, even though the translators of most English versions have adopted it. They reasoned, apparently, that the point of Qoheleth is that nothing is left for mankind but to try to calmly enjoy the present. The present is all that is left to man. The best that man can do is to get some physical pleasure out of life while he can. But as Leupold argues,[2] the only translation of verse 24 that is in harmony with verses 25-26 and that properly leads into chapter 3 is: "There is not a good [that is inherent] in man." There is simply not a comparative statement being made in verse 24, but a statement about what is, or is not, a residual entity within mortals themselves.

---

2     Herbert C. Leupold, *Exposition of Ecclesiastes* (Columbus, OH: Wartburg, 1952), pp. 75-6.

Neither is the preposition (Hebrew *be;* unique in this formula) in the phrase "There is not a good [inherent] *in* man" (emphasis added) to be equated with a different preposition (Hebrew *le,* "for") in 6:12 and 8:15.

Thus we must conclude that even the most mundane and earthly things of life do not lie within a man's grasp to achieve for himself by his own endeavors. The source of all good, contrary to the expectations of most systems of humanism and idealism, cannot be located in man. "One doesn't have it" in one's self, as the saying goes. It is all beyond all of us. Rather, it must come from God. Mortals must get accustomed to realizing that if one is to receive satisfaction from one's food and drink, that satisfaction, like all joyous gifts, will have to come from the hand of God.

Verse 25 reaffirms the principle that "apart from me/him," no one is able to eat or enjoy anything. Some versions read "apart from *me,*" (i.e., many Hebrew texts do in fact have *mimmenni,* "apart from me"), that is, as if it spoke of the laborer in the first person: "Who but I should be first to enjoy my labors?" But eight Hebrew manuscripts, the early Greek translation (Septuagint), the Coptic version, the Syriac, and Jerome's Vulgate all read "apart from *him,*" that is, God. This meaning also fits the context best and is not as awkward as is the first-person rendering. Thus, the situation is as Delitzsch concluded:

> In enjoyment man *is* not free; it depends not on his own will: labor and enjoyment of it do not stand in a necessary connection; but enjoyment is a gift which God imparts.[3]

---

3  Franz Delitzsch, *Commentary on the Song of Songs and Ecclesiastes, trans. M. G. Easton* (1877; reprinted in Commentary on the Old Testament, by C. F. Keil and Franz Delitzsch, Grand Rapids: Eerdmans, 1950), p. 253.

What, then, is the basis on which God distributes His goods and His gift of enjoyment to men? Verse 26 presents that ground. So unexpected is the message of the verse in the eyes of some interpreters that they attribute this verse to a pious writer who added it on his own. How, they ask, can a verse that argues that the good things of life come to those who please God be fitted into the general argument of the rest of the book? This view, they complain, is too cheerful about the state of affairs of life to sit easily with the book's general argument.

But verse 26 merely substantiates the second statement found in verse 24; namely, that the gift of eating and drinking and getting satisfaction from one's work is from the hand of God. The basis of this award is "pleasing God." The opposite of being a God-pleaser is being "one who continues to live in sin." The same contrast between being pleasing to God and being a "sinner" is found in 7:26 and 8:12-13. Those two characteristics are also carefully defined: a sinner is "one who does not fear God," and thus he is "an evil doer," whereas the man pleasing God will fear Him and do good.

Now to this God-pleaser are granted wisdom, knowledge, and joy as divine gifts. All three are gifts, and joy is last in the order, for it is the real turning point and perhaps the most emphasized point of this section. Previously the writer had viewed wisdom, knowledge, and joy separately and by themselves as possible keys to satisfaction and meaning in life (1:16-17; 2:1). But since they were not received as gifts from God and in the context of "pleasing" Him, that is, fearing and serving Him, he had judged them at that time to be "a vexation of spirit" (1:17) and "transitory" (2:1) in their abiding value.

Was this [the gift from God] also ... "transitory and a weariness of spirit"? Hardly. In verse 26, the reference is to the frustrating activity of the *sinner*, who is also divinely given a task. But in his case the task was a troublesome business of gathering and amassing, only to lose it to those who pleased God. All too often some wealthy men have accumulated such huge estates that their heirs were not even able to pay the taxes on the massive numbers of buildings and grounds, so that they were sold or donated to charitable organizations as a tax write-off, or were given outright to Christian institutions or charity. Commentators incorrectly say the referent of "this also is *hebel*" is precisely the three gifts of "wisdom, knowledge, and joy," but how in anybody's view can God's gifts to mortals be classified as so much "vapor," or as being as transitory as "mist, and as elusive as blowing of the wind"?

Mortals in general, for all their so-called puzzling and vexatious toil in accumulating as much as they can in as brief a time as possible, often see their wealth afterward converted to other uses than what they had envisioned it to be in its final state. If only the sinner would come to know God, and if only that one would then receive from God the ability to enjoy the possession of all things, then that person too could experience God's joy and see the good God was doing in this world. In his or her hopes of finding joy in the security of owning what each has carefully stored up around themselves, the final stroke of irony is, and always will be, that the sinner will be forever cut off from that one possession dearer than all others—that is from *joy* itself.

Solomon's experience is conclusive on this point; few persons have exceeded the bounds of such massive possessions as he had; yet they, too, lacked happiness, wisdom, and knowledge as Solomon did when he began "living in sin"—so argued the conclusion to the first section of Ecclesiastes.

In coming to this conclusion, Solomon sets forth five arguments that are contained in the five subdivisions in chapters one and two that precede the concluding verses:

A.   1:3-11—The Stability of Nature and the Transience of We Who Are Mortals

B.   1:12-18—The Search for Wisdom as Our Answer

C.   2:1-11—The Search for the Joy in Our Work

D.   2:12-16—The Examination of the Advantage of Wisdom Over Folly for Us

E.   2:17-23—A Provisional Summary to Our Search Thus Far

F.   2:24-26—Conclusion

## A. 1:3-11 — The Stability of Nature and the Transience of We Who Are Mortals

<sup>3</sup>What does a person gain for all one's labor at which one toils under the sun?

<sup>4</sup>A generation comes and a generation goes, yet the earth remains forever.

<sup>5</sup>The sun rises and the sun sets, then hurries to the place where it arises [again].

<sup>6</sup>The wind blows to the south and turns to the north, round and round the wind keeps going, yet the wind always returns to its course.

⁷All the rivers flow into the sea, yet the sea does not overflow. To the place from which the streams flow, there they return again.

⁸All words are wearisome; more than one can express; the eye never has enough of seeing, nor the ear its fill of hearing.

⁹What has been is what will be, and what has been done is what will be again; there is nothing new under the sun.

¹⁰Is there anything of which it may be said, "Look! this is new?" Already it was here, long ago; it was here before our time!

¹¹There is no lasting remembrance of former [persons], and even those yet to come will not be remembered by those coming after them.

The Teacher's rhetorical question (so typical of wisdom literature) opens this section and sets the tone for the whole book: "What does a person gain for all one's labors at which one toils under the sun?" The word "profit" or "gain" appears in this book only fourteen times. The Greek Septuagint translation rendered *perisseia*, "surplus." Some think this verse asks the question, "What *advantage* does one get from all their toil under the sun?"

Most commentators on Ecclesiastes see this question as the key problem that the whole book seeks to address. Unfortunately, that same majority of commentators incorrectly answer that the "gains, advantages," or "profits" were simply: "Nothing!" They think that *hebel* (1:2) means that everything is so "empty," so "absurd," and so "meaningless" that the only proper response to this rhetorical question is a completely negative answer. What a conclusion for a divine revelation from God! If this were so, perhaps the book should have stopped right at this point, don't you think?

That is why Mr. Fobert has so succinctly concluded, "...why did he [Solomon] bother to continue writing the book, if everything is empty and meaningless[?] For if all of life is that 'absurd,' -- end of discussion; end of book!"[4] However, contrary to such a negative conclusion, the writer went on to give a much more positive outlook in the chapters that followed.

But notice again what happens if in 1:2 the translation of *hebel* is changed from "vanity, emptiness," or "meaninglessness" to the more accurate sense of "mist, change, transience," or "puzzling." Now the question can take on a different tone, for now what is in mind is this: "If everything in life is so temporary, so changing, and so un-lasting, what does anyone get for all their hard work?"

Solomon does not answer that question here; he merely poses the question at this point. Later, he will return to this question on four separate occasions, in 3:9; 5:11; 5:16; and 6:8. There he will begin to answer this key question.

One final note about this central question of the book: even though it appears from 1:3 that our Teacher will limit his search to "under the sun," (used twenty-nine times in Ecclesiastes and nowhere else in the Old Testament) it must be remembered that he has the unusual help of divine inspiration and answers from "above the sun!" An alternative expression appears three times: "under the heavens," (1:13; 2:3; 3:1; also in Gen 6:17; Exod. 17:14; Deut 7:24; 9:14). To claim that this meant

---

4    Glenn Fobert. *Mist Translation and Commentary*. Unpublished, private copy, November 2005, p. 16.

that our Teacher deliberately restricted himself only to what could be observed "under the sun" would mean that his advice could rise no higher than what any other mortal could offer and that divine revelation played little or no part in the composition of this book. How then could his advice be considered "wise" and in the category of what was "right and true" (Eccles. 12:9, 10)? On the contrary, Solomon sought to show us how we could enjoy what was worthwhile in our temporal life and how we could cope with the ebb and flow of change and with some foggy or puzzling issues after we had assumed that God was in charge and there was purpose in all of existence!

It is also to be noticed that the word "all" (Hebrew *kol*) is found more frequently in this book than in any other OT book. In fact, "all" brackets the whole book in 1:2 and 12:8. "All" appears in almost half (41%) of the 222 verses in this book.[5]

Boldly, Solomon goes first of all to the realm of nature in 1:4-11 to make his first point by taking four examples, the earth, sun, wind (air), and rivers (water), and by contrasting their permanence over against the brevity of human beings' stay on earth. Later, some of the Greek philosophers would point to approximately these same four examples (earth, fire, air, and water) as the four basic building blocks of the universe; but even they were not satisfied with those four, for they wanted to know more: what was the fifth item, the "quintessence" (note the root for "five" in this word) of these four that unified them and brought them all together in that one cohesive building block of the universe?!!

---

5    W. Sibley Towner, "The Book of Ecclesiastes," in *The New Interpreter's Bible*.12 vols. (Nashville, TN: Abingdon Press, 1997), V:278.

The reference to a "generation" coming and going (1:4) one after another is not to be related to the cycles of nature, but to human generations. One group of people is on its way in and another group is passing away, yet the earth seems to remain in place. Therefore, despite all the change seen among mortals, there is one fixed point of permanence: the earth remains—along with the other three elements! Thus, the transitory state of men and women is strikingly contrasted with the continually abiding condition of the earth.

But that does not seem fair. Wasn't man made a little lower than the angels (Ps 8:5)? Yet men and women, not the earth, appear to be in a state of transition! Is this what we mortals gain for all of our labor on this planet? Why should the things in nature seem so enduring compared to the transience of men and women?

R.N. Whybray did not favor the view that the Hebrew *dor*, "generation," denoted a human generation or lifespan, for if it did, he thought, then this passage would be commenting on the "transitoriness of human lives, as seen against the background of the continuing existence of the earth…"[6] He wanted to say that everything was to be understood as changing and being cyclical—humans, including nature! But to achieve this conclusion, one also had to disconnect 1:4 from 1:2-3, which verses Whybray saw as an editorial later insertion that summarized Qoheleth's teaching as a whole.

However, if 1:4 remains connected to 1:2-3, as all the evidence seems to suggest, then Whybray must agree with

---

6    R. N. Whybray, "Ecclesiastes 1:5-7 and the Wonders of Nature," *Journal for the Study of the Old Testament* 41(1981):105, and reprinted in Roy B. Zuck, *Reflecting with Solomon: Selected Studies on the Book of Ecclesiastes* (Grand Rapids: Baker, 1994), p. 234.

the point we are making for exactly the reason he wanted to avoid! One (the world of nature) is continuing while the other (human beings) is passing away. The earth remained, but mortals were subject to a lot of change.

The use of the four elements of the earth, sun, wind, and rivers, contrary once again to the conclusions of the majority of the commentators, does not depict the monotony and futility of life, in which the sun, wind, and rivers keep going on in an endless routine day after day, week after week, and year after year. True, their movement is constant, even if it is also somewhat predictable. But it is precisely this factor of constancy and stability in the midst of all this action of movement and motion that is being lamented in this contrast. The sun returns to rise another day and the winds, though often changing, still have a prevailing direction in most regions of the earth. So there is a reliability factor for all of nature in the midst of all this change. That is because God made the world and it contains the purpose He placed in His creation. Therefore, while some aspects of these four elements are puzzling and confusing, there are parts that exhibit constancy and stability. It would be wrong to connect verses 3-11 with the classical Greek myth of Sisyphus, who never quite gets the stone up the hill as it repeatedly rolls down just as the top of the hill is in sight. Solomon's point is not that life is a treadmill filled with monotony.

Some argue, however, that the sun (1:5) is "weary," "pants," or "gasps" (Hebrew *sha'ap*), as if in pain, but beyond some examples of such a meaning (Isa 42:14; Jer 14:6), elsewhere this term depicts an "eagerness" or a "desire" (Ps 119:131; Job 7:2) of the sun to "hurry" on its way. It speeds back to the place where it started the day before, only to arise once more.

Likewise, the wind in 1:6 might appear to some as being aimless, and monotonous, but that was not the point of Qoheleth, the Teacher. Instead, as Whybray noted, "…the wind also has its own fixed circuit and can be relied on to remain within it, always returning (*shab*) eventually to the direction from which it started…."[7] In the same way the rivers never flood the seas into which they empty, for the process of evaporation sucks the water from the seas back into the clouds from which the water rains on the earth to fill the rivers once again.

Instead of these illustrations depicting the *futility* of the natural phenomena, the Teacher declares that "all words" are just plain inadequate and full of labor (not as usually rendered in 1:8—"all *things*" are wearisome) to describe all that is going on in the world around men and women. Most also render *yege'im* as "weary" or "wearisome," but the noun form of this verb occurs much more frequently with the meaning of "labor." Moreover, the word *dabarim*, which is treated by most as "things," is also fairly rendered as "words" in many other similar contexts. In fact, one's eyes or ears can never get enough of observing how nature operates.

In all these statements about nature, the problem remains: their existence appears to be permanent and their courses seem regular and sustained for the most part. But that raises two questions: Aren't there some really new things that appear from time to time (1:10)? And what about mortals that have preceded us: doesn't anyone remember who they were or what they have done (1:11)?

The answer to both questions for the moment seems to be: "No, not really." All the so-called new stuff, if you are

---

7    Whybray, *op.cit*. p. 109; Zuck, *ibid*., p. 237.

thinking about the social, economic, or political fields, has already gone through a number of changes. And the persons who were responsible for many of these human works have long since been forgotten.

So what is the point? Must we conclude that there is more uniformity and stability in nature than there is among mortals? Yes! Why? Because there is "mist, fog, change, transition," and much that "puzzles" us—"apart from God" and His purposes and plans for those who fear Him!

## B. 1:12-18 — The Search for Wisdom as Our Answer

[12]I, the Teacher, have been king over Israel in Jerusalem.

[13]And I decided to devote myself to seek and search out by wisdom all that is done under heaven. What a busy task God has given to the sons of men to keep them occupied!

[14]I have seen all the work which is done under the sun, and behold, all is transitory and a vexation of the spirit.

[15]"What is crooked is not able to be straightened. What is deficient cannot be counted."

[16]I thought to myself, "Look, I have become great and have increased in wisdom more than all who were before me in Jerusalem and I have experienced much wisdom and knowledge."

[17]Thus I applied myself to understand wisdom, and to understand foolishness and folly. I perceived that even this is a striving of spirit.

[18]For with much wisdom comes much grief; the one who increases knowledge is the one adding more pain.

With the uniformity and constancy of sequences in the natural realm established over against the transitoriness and impermanence of mortals who are attempting to make sense of these puzzling facts, Solomon now turns to speak to us in the first person, which he will use throughout most of the rest of the book. He will offer his own situation in a more general way in verses 12-18 and then he will do so in a more detailed way in 2:1-11. Other than King David and King Solomon, of no other Davidic king could it be said that they ruled over all Israel (1:12).

Solomon continued his search for what it is that a person gains for all his living and working on this earth. Since he had been uniquely gifted by God with "wisdom," this section of 1:12-18 raises another question: what about education? What does God, who is in heaven, have to do with man who is on earth? What does "under the sun" have to do with "above the sun?" Does the fear of God have anything to do with human culture and secular thought?

The word "wisdom" appears in verses 13, 16 (twice), 17, and again in 18. Roland Murphy[8] also viewed the structure of these verses as two similar sections supported by one proverb each:

> Verses 12-14—On pursuing wisdom
>
> Proverb offered in support—v. 15
>
> Verses 16-17—More on pursuing wisdom
>
> Proverb offered in support—v. 18

Viewed from another similar perspective, 1:12-18 is a sort of double introduction to the book after the question of 1:2-3 has been posed and briefly illustrated in a counter-point way in 1:4-11. This double introduction may be divided as

---

8    Roland Murphy. *Wisdom Literature. Forms of Old Testament Literature* (Grand Rapids: Eerdmans, 1981), vol. 13, p. 134.

Addison G. Wright suggested: (a) 1:12-15, with verse 15 as an accompanying proverb to close the unit; (b) 1:16-18, with verse 18 as an accompanying proverb to close the unit. Furthermore, Wright believed that there is a partial A-B, B-A form (*chiasmus*) in these two introductions:

> A. "I applied my mind" (v. 13), i.e., "I devoted myself..."
>
> B. "I have seen everything" (v. 14).
>
> B. "I have acquired great wisdom...my mind has had great experience" (vv. 16-17).
>
> A. "I applied my mind" (v. 17).[9]

At the least, "I applied my mind" (vv. 13 and 17, or "I devoted myself" or "I applied myself…") is what is known as an inclusion (a sort of bracketing off of material by beginning and ending a section).

Now if Solomon did indeed compose this treatise of Ecclesiastes for a mixed audience of Israelites and Gentiles, who, like the Queen of Sheba, came from afar to sample his wisdom, then his message and examples would be adapted to the level of his audience. And if Solomon is going to give advice, he must first state his qualifications for pursuing the proposed inquiry: "What gain (or advantage) is there in this life for a mortal?"

Simply stated, his qualifications included:

- He had been ruling (or "I was ruling," as a past tense, or a present perfect, "I still am ruling") as king over all Israel in Jerusalem (v. 12).

---

9    Addison G. Wright, "The Riddle of the Sphinx: The Structure of the Book of Qoheleth," *Catholic Biblical Quarterly* 30 (1968): 326.

- He had diligently applied himself to answer this question (v. 13).

- He had carefully observed all that pertained to this question (v. 14).

- He had acquired more wisdom and knowledge than most other people (v. 16).

- He found much grief and sorrow in things as they were (v. 17).

The careful reader will notice, as we said on verse 12, that Qoheleth has now switched from the third person of 1:1-2 ("The words of Qoheleth, the Teacher, Assembler [of the people], son of David, king in Jerusalem") to the first person ("I, the Teacher/Assembler [of the people], was king in Jerusalem" [1:12]). As we saw in the introduction, 1:12 can easily be translated, "I, Qoheleth, *have been* king in Jerusalem" up to this time. If any man could unlock the mysteries in this topic, it would be someone such as this famed wise man from Jerusalem to whom God had given such a wonderful gift of wisdom.

Solomon plunged enthusiastically into the investigation. He "searched" (from a Hebrew word meaning "to seek the roots of a matter") and "explored" (the Hebrew literally meaning "to investigate a subject on all sides")[10] all things done under heaven. In all candor, he records that he found the task a "sore travail" ("difficult business" or "sorry task") that God (this is the first time *Elohim*, "God," is mentioned in the book) had given to "the sons of the man" (Hebrew has "*Adam*" or "man," not "men").

10 George A. Barton, *A Critical and Exegetical Commentary on the Book of Ecclesiastes* (1908; reprinted in *The International Critical Commentary*, edited by Samuel R. Driver, Alfred Plummer, and Charles A. Briggs, Edinburgh: T. & T. Clark, 1959), p. 78.

Was Solomon thereby alluding to Adam and the effects of the Fall? Yes, that seems to be the situation. He did not choose to say "sons of *men*," but instead, "the sons of Adam" labor and toil without finding any satisfaction or an answer to the question: What is the profit or gain to mortals? Yet all the time it was God who continued to prompt man's heart to discover the truth.

The Teacher began by referring to his royal position. This was significant, for if life on earth could offer anything good, it ought to be available to the king above all others. The king not only had the gift of wisdom, but he also had a wide and extensive view of all that is done under heaven, especially in light of his having access to the international trade routes and his concourse with the peoples that came from distant lands as well. His use of the suffixial (or preterite) form of the verb (*hayiti*, "I was king") is not an argument against Solomonic authorship, as we have argued already, for this form of the Hebrew verb is often used for a past that stretches into the present: "I have been king...."

The Teacher's efforts to investigate all things came up with dismal results. He did not begin with preconceived notions as to how things ought to be; instead, he traced and followed his facts as closely as he could. "Wisdom" is the catchword in this section, and thus it is with good reason that the Hebrew form of *hokmah*, "wisdom," is shown with the article in verse 13. Therefore, Solomon carried out his search with the instrument of wisdom. What was the profit or advantage in all of this, was still the question. Man was trapped by the difficulty of the problem and his own divinely implanted hunger to know the answer. It was a very tricky business indeed. From the wealth of his personal observation and interviews with men and women of every calling, from all sorts of foreign lands, Solomon's conclusion is almost brutal. The "good" and "profit" that any part of this world has to offer is this: "All is transitory and a vexation of spirit/blowing of the wind," i.e., it is vexing to the spirit of human beings (v. 14). Creation has truly been subjected to "transition." Size the world up as one may, it still comes out to the same brief result.

For one who has achieved an international reputation as a wise man, his conclusions must carry all the more weight. The words of 1:16-18 are best rendered as TEV translated them, "The wiser you are, the more worries you have; the more you know, the more it hurts." All Solomon's wisdom, if that is all one must go on, was *hebel*, a changing puff of "mist," a "gathering fog," a "puzzle" indeed.

The proverb in verse 15 speaks of the general character of human affairs, as allowed by God, so that all who seek satisfaction by all of these earthly means are left with despair. Verse 15 defines in what sense the conclusion of the preceding verse is to be understood. No investigation, the concluding proverb of verse 15 maintains, is going to be able to make up what is deficient and lacking from anything in this world. So much is lacking that it boggles the mind to even try to count it up. Neither can all that is crooked, twisted, perverted, and turned upside down be set right and put in order, given merely the materials at hand in this world. However, Solomon's proverb is applied too broadly if he is understood to be claiming that there is no use trying to change anything ever because nothing can ever be straightened out and the deficiencies are too numerous ever to be patched. Rather, the proverb summarizes the fruit of Solomon's search on a horizontal, terrestrial plane alone. The problem calls for a solution greater than the sum of all its parts. It calls for the intervention of God.

Once again, as if to introduce the book anew, Solomon repeats in 1:16 his qualifications to conduct the search for an answer to the question of 1:3: What is the use of trying to work on anything? In pondering the issue, he notes for his reader's appreciation, the position from which he answers their plaintive cry. "Look," he says, "I have grown great" in wealth and dignity. Furthermore, "My mind has had great experience in wisdom and knowledge." In an attempt to let contraries explain each other, he pondered folly as well as wisdom.

The result was again put in a proverb in verse 18: Wisdom, when viewed apart from that wisdom which comes from the fear of God (which he eulogizes in 2:13-14; 5:7; 7:18; 8:12; 12:13, and other wisdom texts such as Job 28:28; Ps 111:10; Prov 15:33), only increases grief instead of bringing relief to the question of profit. This is proud, human wisdom, says Ginsburg, which "Dethrones God and deifies man, pretending to give him laws and regulations whereby to make him happy."[11]

## C. 2:1-11 — The Search for the Joy in Our Work

After Solomon had completed his list of qualifications to speak to this question in a sort of double introduction (1:3-11; 1:14-18), with two proverbs in the second of the two introductions that set forth his results in a general and preliminary way, he now elucidates more specifically what proofs and tests he used to come to this conclusion. Using a form of a monologue (such as can be found in Psalms 42:5, 11; 43:5 or Luke 12:19: "I will say to my soul: soul, you have many goods…", NKJV), Solomon investigated the "gain" or "profit" of the following areas of his life:

---

11    Ginsburg, p. 275.

Mirth and Joy—vv. 1-3

Building and Land Improvements—vv. 4-6

Possessions and Music—vv. 7-8

[1] I said to myself, "Come now, I will conduct a test about joy and learn what is good. But behold, this too was puzzling.

[2] "Laughter," I said, "was foolish. And Joy [itself], what does joy accomplish?"

[3] I tried cheering my mind and my body with wine, while my mind was still guiding [me] with wisdom and taking hold of folly, until I could see what was good for the sons of men to do under heaven—counting the days of their lives.

[4] I made for myself great projects: I built houses for myself and I planted vineyards for myself.

[5] I made gardens and parks for myself, and I planted in them trees of every kind of fruit.

[6] I made for myself reservoirs of water to irrigate groves of flourishing trees.

[7] I acquired male and female slaves and had slaves who were born in my house. Also, [I acquired] a large number of herds and flocks, more than any who were before me in Jerusalem.

[8] I amassed for myself silver and gold, the treasure of kings and provinces. I put together for myself male and female choirs—the delights of the sons of men, and many mistresses.[12]

---

12   The meaning of the Hebrew *shiddah weshiddoth* is very uncertain. Some render it as "concubines," but Hebrew has a correct word for them, *pilgesh*. "Mistress(es)" usually applied to a woman with female servants (e.g., Gen. 16:8), but in those cases they use a different word than *shiddah* (Craig G. Bartholomew. *Ecclesiastes*. Grand Rapids: Baker, 2009, p. 129, n. 11).

[9]I became great and surpassed anyone who was before me in Jerusalem; also my wisdom remained with me.

[10]And all that my eyes desired I did not refuse them; I did not restrain my heart from any joy. For my heart rejoiced in all my labor, and this was my reward from all my toil.

[11]But then I surveyed all the work my hands had accomplished and the effort I had exerted in doing it; and behold, all was temporary and a vexation of spirit, and there was no profit under the sun.

While many commentators use the English translation of "pleasure" to interpret the Hebrew *simchah*, which most often is rendered "joy," or "rejoicing," even in other parts of Ecclesiastes, we prefer to stick with "joy" in 2:1. Therefore, Solomon is not referring to hedonistic pleasure or mirth, but to the same joy mentioned in 9:7, which joy comes from the Lord Himself.

Does that mean, then, that enjoyment is also illusory and a mist—like a fog? Most would have thought that the joy of the Lord lasts forever. But even here, a caution must be raised. Happiness is not the sole or main purpose of life, nor is it one unending series of joyful happenings with nothing else intervening. Joy in life must be tempered with weeping (Rom. 12:15). Rejoicing is a significant part of life, but this is not the only emotion.

Nevertheless, note with what hilarity and laughter must the palace halls have echoed as Solomon, his courtiers, and his guests exchanged jokes, drank wine, listened to the witty merrymakers from all over the region, and feasted bountifully *each day* (as I Kings 4:20-23 will inform us) on "thirty measures of fine flour, sixty measures of meal, ten fat oxen, twenty oxen from the pastures, one hundred sheep, in addition to harts, roebucks, fallow deer and fattened fowl" (1 Kings 4:22-23)! Some estimates suggest that it would take thirty or forty thousand people to consume that much food each day. No wonder 1 Kings 4:20 says, "Judah and Israel were as many as the sand which is by the sea in multitude, all eating and drinking, and making merry" (KJV). The whole plan was to sample the joy and fun of life until he could determine what was "good" for the sons of man (again, it appears as sons of Adam).

Without telling us the results, he passes immediately to an account of his vast building and land improvements. As for himself, he devoted thirteen years to building "the king's house" (1 Kings 9:10). Then he built "the house of the forest of Lebanon" (1 Kings 10:17), and another house for his wife, Pharaoh's daughter. He also built the cities of Hazor, Megiddo, Gezer, Beth-horon, Baalath, and Tadmor in the wilderness.

Solomon also moved into horticulture, gardening, and the nursery business (2:5-6). In doing so he carried out the original cultural mandate given to man in the Garden of Eden: he was to cultivate, work, and guard it, i.e., the natural world that had come from the hand of the Creator. (Note, as Ginsburg[13] pointed out, that the Hebrew word for *vineyard* [*gan*] is from *ganan,* meaning "to guard." So we see that the job of protecting is reflected also in the German [*Garten*] and English [*garden*] words for the same concept.)

The pools of water used to irrigate his young trees may be the traditional pools of Solomon which are located several miles southwest of Jerusalem in the Valley of Artas, though not mentioned in Scripture as being built by Solomon. There, according to Robinson (as cited by Ginsburg), "Huge reser-

---

13  Ginsburg, *op. cit.*

voirs built of squared stones and bearing marks of the highest antiquity" were set in a steep part of the valley. The three pools, measured in feet, had the following sizes:

|        | Length | Breadth | Depth |
|--------|--------|---------|-------|
| Lower  | 582    | 207     | 50    |
| Middle | 423    | 250     | 39    |
| Upper  | 380    | 236     | 25    |

To these improvements, Solomon added many possessions (vv. 7-9). An account of Solomon's riches appears in 1 Kings 10:14-29. According to some estimates (taking a talent of gold to be worth approximately fifteen hundred un-inflated dollars), his annual income was over one million dollars in purchasing power. Rare and curious things, distinctive to kings and kingdoms, were amassed by Solomon's fleets returning from Ophir (1 Kings 9:26-28). So great was his fortune that silver and gold were soon to be regarded in Jerusalem as paving stones (1 Kings 10:27; 2 Chron. 1:15). In fact, he owned whatever he looked on, and his looks went everywhere, with apologies to Browning's "My Last Duchess."

Since the Teacher had concluded that wisdom and reason alone do not satisfy in the last section, he turns in this section to see if wisdom and wealth will make a difference. The literary style he will use in this section is the device of simulating a conversation with himself (2:1)—indeed, a monologue.[14]

But he concludes here too that the worth of all this acquiring and building had to be evaluated much as he had concluded in the previous section, where he had

---

14  Note once again the pleonastic use of the pronoun *ani*, "I," presumably for emphasis.

studied wisdom, madness, and folly in 1:16-18. What was the advantage and profit (1:3) of this labor as well, he wondered? The answer remained the same—there was no advantage! Something was sadly missing. Not one of all those good things had brought satisfaction or joy.

## D. 2:12-16 — The Examination of the Advantage of Wisdom Over Folly for Us

Solomon, apparently dissatisfied with what he had accomplished in his previous experiments, revisits wisdom, madness, and folly once again. This time he wants to know, "What can a man do, who comes after the king, except what has already been done?"

> [12]So I myself turned to consider wisdom and madness and folly. For what can a man do who comes after the king, but what has already been done?
>
> [13]Then I saw that there is an advantage of wisdom over folly, just as there is an advantage of light over darkness.
>
> [14]The wise person has his eyes in his head, but the fool walks in darkness. Yet I myself realized that one happening occurs to all of them.
>
> [15]I said to myself in my heart, "As happens to the fool, so it will happen even to me; why then have I been excessively wise?" So I said to myself, "This too is puzzling/transient."
>
> [16]For there is no lasting remembrance of the wise one or the fool; already the days are coming when everything will be forgotten. How does the wise person die? Just like the fool!

Few, if any, could rival Solomon in his possessions, building projects, or the like. But if this were true, then lesser mortals' quest to find real profit in life from life itself seemed to be a hopeless task. The value of life and its profit had to lie in other avenues. But Solomon wants to retrace his steps and look one more time at wisdom, madness, and folly.

It did become clear (v. 13), however, that wisdom was vastly superior to any of the acquisitions or pleasures secured from things. The benefit of wisdom over folly was comparable to that of light over darkness. The wise man could see farther ahead and in many directions (his "eyes are in his head" [v. 14]), yet was this obvious "advantage" (*yitron,* cf. 1:3) a permanent one? Could wisdom also insulate us from the attack of death?

The sad answer was "no." "One event" (rather than rendering this word *miqreh,* also *yiqreh,* appearing seven of its ten Biblical instances in Ecclesiastes alone, as "fate," "chance," or "destiny") overtakes both the fool and the wise man—death (v. 15). Both die, and both are forgotten by men (v. 16). Life in itself did not provide such gains as to answer the question of what "advantage" (Hebrew *yitron,* "gain," same word as in 1:3) there was in life itself. If this were all there was, the wise man and the fool would die alike and both alike would be forgotten—in which case life was a cheat and a delusion (v. 17). All the labor spent in acquiring wisdom gave little if any ultimate advantage.

## E. 2:17-23 — A Provisional Summary to Our Search Thus Far

The Teacher seems to fall into a serious state of mind as it appears he now contradicts, in verse 17, what he just said in 2:10. There he had said that his heart rejoiced in his work, but now he claimed that his work was grievous to him. How could that be a good theological conclusion? And how will he get to the high conclusion we have already looked at in 2:24-26? Let us translate the text first and then we shall examine it.

[17]Therefore, I came to dislike life because the work that is done under the sun was grievous to me; for all is temporary and a vexation of spirit/blowing in the wind.

[18]And I even[15] disliked all my toil, which I had labored for under the sun, because I must leave it to someone who would be after me.

[19]Who knows whether he will be a wise person or a fool? Yet he shall rule over all my labor which I have toiled over and by which I have acted wisely under the sun. This also is a puzzle.

[20]Therefore my heart began to despair over all the labor which I had done under the sun.

[21]For there is a person whose toil is in wisdom and in knowledge, and with skill; yet to the person who has not toiled in it, he will leave it for his portion; this also is puzzling and a great evil.

[22]For what does a person get for all his toil and for the vexation of his heart, which he will labor under the sun?

[23]For all his days are a pain, and his task grief; even in the night his heart did not rest. This too is puzzling.

The Hebrew verb *sane'ti,* "I hated" may be more like "I came to dislike."[16] As T.A. Perry noted in that same place:

The verb covers a wide range of emotion, from deep disgust to simple negation, rather than [it being a] contradiction, of 'love' (thus 'unloved, disliked' rather than 'hatred'); cf. Deut. 21:15; Judg. 14:16. At any rate, K. [Koheleth] does

---

15    T.A. Perry [*Dialogues with Kohelet: The Book of Ecclesiastes: Translation and Commentary* (University Park, PA: The Pennsylvania State University Press, 1993), p. 82] commented that the emphatic "I" pronoun stresses his "hatred" to an even more radical level.

16    Ibid., p. 82.

come to hate life to the extent that he wishes to leave it, as does Job (6:8-9).

If wealth and wisdom are both dead-end trails in this search, perhaps there is satisfaction in laying up wealth for others or for one's children. Regrettably, that also is no solution. There is no way of knowing whether that inheritance will be used wisely or foolishly (vv. 18-21).

So Solomon concludes this first section as he began it: "What is there to a mortal?" (2:22; = "what advantage is there to a person?" [1:3]). Day and night he has seen only toil of body and mind. A mortal does not possess anything within or outside him or herself to aid one in securing permanent happiness.

Only now are we prepared to receive Solomon's hard-hitting summary.

## F. 2:24-26 — Conclusion

- There is nothing (inherently) good in a person *per se*.

- No one can really appreciate even such elementary

- things as eating and drinking apart from a personal relationship with the living God.

- God alone—not things or wisdom—is the giver of satisfaction and joy.

- God also gives wisdom, knowledge, and joy to those who please Him.

In contrast to this, how far off the mark is every other pursuit. The question of 1:3, as to what does life in and of itself profit a person can now be answered.

[24]There is nothing [inherently] good in a person [to enable one] to eat, drink and cause one's soul to see good in one's labor. Even this, I myself realized, was from the hand of God.

[25]For apart from him [God], who can eat and who can find enjoyment?

[26]For to the person who is pleasing before him, he [God] gives wisdom, knowledge and joy; but to the sinner he gives the task of gathering and amassing [things or wealth?], [only] to give to one who is pleasing in God's sight. This too is a puzzle/transitory and a vexation of spirit.

The conclusion to this first section is found in 2:24-26: the purpose of life cannot be found in and of itself for any one of the good things found in the world. All the things that we call the "goods" of life—health, riches, possessions, position, sensual pleasures, honors, and prestige—slip through one's hands unless they are received as a gift from God. Until God gives persons the ability to enjoy them and obtain satisfaction from them, they simply cannot in and of themselves compensate for the joy that comes from fearing God and knowing Him. God gives that ability to those who begin by "fearing," that is, believing, Him. (See the later discussion of "fear" at 8:12-13.) There is where joy begins and continues—in God Himself.

# 2

# UNDERSTANDING THE ALL-ENCOMPASSING PLAN OF GOD

*Ecclesiastes 3:1–5:20*

Solomon's personal experience as king, and the restlessness of nature itself, laid the groundwork for the inescapable conclusion that if enjoyment and happiness were ever going to be within anyone's reach, they would need to come as direct gifts from God to persons of faith—so Solomon taught by divine revelation. The wicked, meanwhile, were left with the aggravating and empty task of accumulating goods that could soon be converted to other uses by those fearing God as the wicked yielded those things up at their death. The contrast and difference in the outcome of each is very explicit in this memorable section of Ecclesiastes.

Thus, in the next step in his fourfold argument in this book of Ecclesiastes, Solomon boldly argued the thesis that every action of an individual can be traced to its ultimate source, which is an all-embracing plan that is administered by God (3:1). This is a beautiful plan, yet men and women do not and, as a matter of fact, cannot apprehend it because of their prevailing worldliness. So vast, so eternal, and so comprehensive in its inclusions is this plan that mortals are both threatened and exasperated in their attempts to discover it for themselves. Nevertheless, being built by God, and being made in God's own image, each person possesses a hunger within his or her heart to know the vastness, wholeness, and key details of this plan. Yet it cannot be known until one comes to personally know the living God (3:11). Therefore, each is once again cut off from the very substance for which his or her whole being yearns, just as each likewise searched for happiness and joy in chapters 1 and 2. There must be a divine plan behind all of this!

## VIEWING THE CALL FOR US TO UNDERSTAND THE ALL-ENCOMPASSING PLAN OF GOD FROM THE CONCLUSION OF THE SECTION — ECCLESIASTES 5:18-20 (HEBREW 17-19)

[18](17H) Look! Here is what I realized: it is good and beautiful/fitting for one to eat, to drink, and to see goodness in all his toil which he has done under the sun during the days God has given him; for this is his reward.

[19](18H) Furthermore, when God gives any person wealth and riches, and empowers him to enjoy them, and to accept them as his portion and to rejoice in his toil; this is a gift of God.

[20](19H) For he will not long brood over the days of his life, for God will keep him busy [or continuously answers] with [through] the joy in his heart.

W. Sibley Towner commented that:

These next verses [5:18-20], in contrast, bring the passage to a close with a reprise (see 2:24-26) of the only consistently positive theme of the book: that the proper goal of all human endeavor is joy. A good life of enjoyment of the fruits of human labor is possible if people will simply look on food, drink, and money as gifts from God and accept their 'lot' [(*heleq*) v. 18; cf. 2:10, 'reward'; 3:22)].[1]

Therefore, as we did with the first section of chapters one and two, it will be best to begin our investigation of chapters three to five with the writer's conclusion to the section as we attempt to assess the development of the principle that God has an all-embracing plan that covers all persons, times, and actions. Thus we propose to judge the whole section of 3:1– 5:17 in light of its intended goal in 5:18-20. The following list is a fair appraisal of the writer's conclusion to the second part of his work.

- God's proposed course of living is "good," that is, without moral problems (v. 18a).

- God's plan can also be declared to be an "appropriate," "beautiful," or "fitting" path to tread. It possesses aesthetic and practical qualities, along with its moral perfections (v. 18b).

- Enjoyment, not worldly accumulations, is the principal end to be sought. Therefore, neither the plan of God nor religion was ever meant to stifle our pleasure and joy in possessing things or our joy in life itself (v. 18c).

- In fact, the man who has learned the secret of enjoyment as a gift from God will not become anxious over the length of his life. He has too much joy in living to "brood over" the impermanence of his mortal being.

---

1    W. Sibley Towner, "Ecclesiastes," in *The New Interpreter's Bible*. Leander E. Keck, ed. (Nashville, TN: Abingdon, 1997), vol. 5, p.319.

Rather, each day is taken as it comes, as a gift from God (vv. 18d-19).[2]

- God himself "answers," or "keeps one occupied" (v. 20b), that is, makes his being to correspond to the joy in one's heart. People are thereby kept occupied and delighted in the inner recesses of their lives with God Himself. Consequently, the dark side of man's brief life is relieved and exchanged for gladness in the plan of God.

Thus we arrive at a similar conclusion to that given in 2:24-26, with the addition that the scheme, or the plan, of life itself is not monotonous or dreary, because it too is in the hands of God. Why then should a person "brood, sulk," or even curse any aspect of God's gift of life, or his promised ability to enjoy everything, no matter how trivial, mundane, or ephemeral in comparison to himself? But let us turn now to the development of the argument.

The structure of this section (3:1–5:17) is more easily described than the previous section of the book, for it moves from the famous poem on appropriate times for everything (3:1-8) to a discussion on God's purposes for life (3:9-15). Surely, this states the general principle of our section, viz.,

---

2    In *The Book of Ecclesiastes* (Grand Rapids: Eerdmans, 1998, p. 168), Tremper Longman III continues his pessimistic view of the book by saying: "…his [Qoheleth's] depressing tone may be heard in the last words of the verse [17], the few days God has given that person, for that is his reward." But T. A. Perry, in *Dialogues with Kohelet* (University Park, PA: Pennsylvania State University Press, 1993, p. 113), seemed to be more on track when he noted, "Despite the general preference for interpretations denoting paucity…the sense here is definitely not pessimistic. Gordis (1968) cites Job 14:5… 'the number of his months,' (where man's days are numbered). However, even this example does not argue limitation in the sense of 'few,' but rather the more relevant sense of a providential determination, a numbering that God performs at birth or from the beginning."

that God does have a plan and that it does embrace every person, in all actions, and in all times of life.

But if that is true, then what are we to say about the anomalies and apparent contradictions to this thesis? Six cases are raised by the Teacher, usually introduced by the rhetorical formula:

"And still I saw…" (3:16),

"Also I thought to myself" [or "I said in my heart"] (3:18),

"I looked again and I saw" [or "Again I turned and saw…"] (4:1),

"[And] I saw" (4:4),

"I looked again and I saw" [or "Again I turned and I saw"] (4:7),

with only 4:13 being without an introductory formula similar to the other five. And what was it that the Teacher saw, which he thought somewhat disrupted his principle that God's plan was all-embracing? The things that seemed to be spoiling the beauty of God's plan were:

| | | |
|---|---|---|
| 1. | 3:16-17 | The courts were unjust |
| 2. | 3:18-21 | Death came to all |
| 3. | 4:1-3 | People were being oppressed |
| 4. | 4:4-6 | People were being envious |
| 5. | 4:7-12 | People were often isolated |
| 6. | 4:13-16 | Popularity was temporary |

If these mitigating "facts" intruded on the success of the plan of God, what implications did the acknowledgement of these anomalies have by way of cautions and warnings for those who feared God and believed that God did have a plan after all? Qoheleth's warning seemed to be that men and women should be careful not to make a hasty miscalculation about all of these anomalies, or apparent contradictions, so that they ended up denying the reality and the existence of God's providence, assuming instead that God Himself did not have a plan that embraced all of reality.

The structure for this second section of the book of Ecclesiastes, then, will be:

A.  3:1-15—The Principle: God's Plan Embraces All of Our Reality

B.  3:16–4:16—The Facts: Anomalies Must Not Be Used by Us to Deny God's Plan

C.  5:1-17—The Implications: Certain Warnings and Cautions to Us are in Order

D.  5:18-20—Conclusion

# A. 3:1-15 – The Principle: God's Plan Embraces All of Our Reality

¹For everything there is a season,
>a time for every matter under heaven:

²a time to give birth, and a time to die;
>a time to plant, and a time to uproot what was planted;

³a time to kill and a time to heal;
>a time to tear down and a time to build;

⁴a time to weep, and a time to laugh;
>a time to mourn, and a time to skip about;

⁵a time to scatter stones, and a time to gather stones;
  a time to embrace, and a time to abstain from embracing;

⁶a time to search, and a time to give up;
  a time to keep and a time to throw away;

⁷a time to rend, and a time to stitch together;
  a time to be silent and a time to speak;

⁸a time to love, and a time to hate;
  a time of war, and a time of peace.

⁹What gain do the workers have for their toil?

¹⁰I have seen the business that God has given to the sons of the men to be occupied with.

¹¹He has made everything beautiful in its time. Moreover he has also set eternity in their hearts, from which a person is not able to find the work God has done from the beginning to the end.

¹²I recognized that there is nothing good in them except to rejoice and to do good while they live.

¹³And also that every person should eat and drink and realize good in all his toil; it is the gift of God.

¹⁴I know that everything that God does will be forever; nothing can be added to it and nothing can be diminished; God does it so that they should fear [be in awe before] him.

¹⁵What is has already been; that which is to be has already been; God seeks what is pursued.

The poem of 3:1-8 may be one of the best-known portions of the Bible to many who often know very little of the rest of the Bible, but it is also at the same time one of the least understood passages. The Teacher's intention here is not directly to make prescriptions for life, but mainly to offer pronouncements on the fact that from the perspective of God, it is He who orders all aspects of a person's life and actions. Even when there is sickness, death, war, and the like, God is in charge of the seasons and times of life. This does not mean God is willing to let a person's life fall into chaos, for He also makes sure there are times for giving birth, healing, and peace as well.

Life is not one of chance or fate, for despite the haphazard *appearance* of things, God alone is in charge of nature and history. The only persons who would be upset by this are secularists who wish to be their own god over all things. Michael Kelley noted that

> The precise quality of man's rebellion lies in his supreme aspiration to make nature and history serve and glorify man. To accomplish that goal he must have the absolute lordship of time and its content.[3]

Kelley went on to quote from Rousas Rushdoony to the same effect:

> In ancient paganism...humanistic man sought to govern time by means of rites whose purpose was to control time and nature. In fertility and chaos cults, men believed they could make nature fruitful again, wipe out past history and sins, reverse time and order, and generate themselves, nature, and history.[4]

Moderns are, more often than not, no less optimistic about reaching the same goals—and doing it all, but deliberately apart or separate from God!

---

3    Michael Kelley. *The Burden of God: Studies in Wisdom and Civilization from the Book of Ecclesiastes* (Minneapolis, MN: Contra Mundum Books, 1993), p. 84.

4    Rousas John Rushdoony. *Revolt Against Maturity* (Fairfax, VA: Thoburn Press, 1977), p. 228.

However, for all the affairs of life, argued Qoheleth, God has set a time, i.e., the length of time ("a season") for everything, v. 1, and the particular events ("a time" for this and "a time" for that) along that time band or "season" where each event is established and ordained in the providence of God. Our times are in God's hands (Ps. 31:15); therefore, what those who fear God must do is to "redeem the time" (Eph. 5:15), for God has made everything "beautiful in its time" (Eccles. 3:11).

To illustrate this broad and comforting assertion, the writer turns to fourteen pairs of opposites in verses 2-8. Twenty-eight times, "time" is repeated as he presses home the point of God's foreordination and man's accountability.

Some (e.g., Leupold)[5] have attempted to interpret these pairs of contrasting events as if they were intended to signify, in an allegorical or spiritualizing way, the church or the nations. The result is a travesty of the meaning intended by the author. It simply cannot be shown that Qoheleth meant by the idea of giving birth to signify moral regeneration; by death, the death of the old, sinful nature of man; by planting, the spiritual implantation of truth in the heart; by uprooting, the destruction of the sin principle in the heart of man; by killing, the mortification of sin; by healing, the recovery from sin; and so on. Nor was the writer limiting or directing his remarks to the birth and death of nations *per se*. (Compare, however, in a different context, Jeremiah 1:10 for the pairs to "plant, uproot" and "build, tear down.")

The references in verses 2-8 are basically to individuals. The plan of God encompassed everything in the lives of

---

5    Herbert C. Leupold, *Exposition of Ecclesiastes* (Columbus, OH: Wartburg, 1952), p. 82.

human beings from the day of our being born to the day of our death. God appointed both our birthday and the day of our funeral. Thus the entirety of human existence encompasses the list of fourteen illustrations of the comprehensiveness of the plan of God.

Next, Qoheleth moves to the vegetable realm and teaches us that even the life of vegetables is set in the scope of God's plan—when they are to be planted and when they are to be uprooted (v. 2). (It may be noted in passing that this pair is also used later in Jeremiah 18:7 and Zephaniah 2:4, among other references, to apply metaphorically to nations.)

Having established that the term of life is fixed for persons as well as for the plant world, Solomon teaches that even those situations that seem to be in the hands of mortals and, therefore, somewhat unpredictable—such as the condemnation of murderers by the state to the penalty of death—are likewise embraced in the plan of God. There is a time for executing murderers or destroying enemies in a just war (v. 3).

Incidentally, such action against murderers is favored in Scripture, not because men and women are sovereign or because society and the bereaved victims are somehow benefited, but because persons are so vastly important to God—they are made in the image of God [Gen. 9:6].) To kill another person with malice and by deliberately lying in wait to do so (first-degree murder) is to kill God in effigy. Thus, when guilt can be demonstrated beyond any reasonable doubt, the only alternative that the state, God's duly authorized agent in such a case, has is to show respect for God and for the value of the image of God in man by taking the murderer's life. Such a moral reason (i.e., people are made in the image of God) has not been antiquated by any subsequent revelation in the gospel. And how could it be antiquated? Can the character of God be offered at discount value in generations to come?

Along with taking life in those designated times, the plan of God includes a time "to heal," or, literally, "to sew," "to heal a wound." Likewise, there is a time to break down old walls, relationships, or even, metaphorically, hostility between nations (e.g., Jer. 18:7, 9), as well as a time to build them up.

Intimately connected with these examples of the antitheses in God's providence are the sorrows and joys that accompany the events described in verses 2-3. Solomon begins in verse 4 with "to weep" (*libkot*), possibly because the Hebrew word sounds so similar to the last word in the preceding set, *libnot* ("to build"). So also "to leap," or "to dance" (*regod*) is probably used instead of "to rejoice" (*semeach*) because it sounds like "to mourn" (*sepod*).[6] Accordingly, divine providence warrants times of laughter, joy, and pleasure as well as the joy of assonance.

This list of attitudes is continued in verse 5, which notes that what was once easily discarded as so many useless stones would on another occasion be earnestly sought out as valuable building materials. Thus men often treat one and the same material or person differently, depending on their condition, needs, and the controlling power of God. Put in proverbial terms, there is a time to embrace (the familiar) and a time to refrain from embracing.

So much for the usual, the common, the familiar in all its forms; but the same thing can be said for man's desire to

---

6    Christian D. Ginsburg, *Coheleth, Commonly Called the Book of Ecclesiastes* [1861]; reprinted in *The Song of Songs and Coheleth (Commonly Called the Book of Ecclesiastes)*, The Library of Biblical Studies, edited by Harry M. Orlinsky (New York: Ktav, 1970), p. 305.

get new things. There are times when mortals should seek new objects (v. 6), even though there will be other times when the same persons will lose some of those earthly treasures. Likewise, along with the acquisition of new properties, there are times for guarding things and times for throwing them away. For example, in verse 7 Solomon applied this contrast to the abandoning and preserving of clothing. When bad news came, it was appropriate in Solomon's time to rip the front of one's garments to display one's grief (2 Sam. 13:31); with the passing of the problem, it was proper to sew the torn clothes together again.

But what happens when the great calamities of life come? Here again, there are times when it is best to remain silent in the heat of adversity (2 Kings 2:3, 5), and there are times when one has to speak and cry out against the evil witnessed, even if to no one else but God (v. 7). Men are placed in situations in which they are stirred to love or are moved to hate. In Psalm 105:25, God "turned" the "hearts" of the Egyptians "to hate" and "to deal craftily" with Israel, whereas previously Israel had enjoyed favor from that same nation under the good hand of God as they asked for jewels (Exod. 11:3). So Solomon concluded the series with the message that there are divinely appointed times for war and peace (v. 8).

Yet the question persisted: What is to be gained from the whole scene? Ecclesiastes 3:9 is but a return to the question of 1:3. The answer is clear. All life unfolds under the appointment of divine providence—birth, death; growth, harvest; joys, sorrows; acquiring, losing; speaking up, being silent; war and peace. Since everything has its time from God, all the labor of a person by itself cannot change the times, circumstances, or control of events.

But 3:10 must be taken together with verse 11. For on further revelation, it must be boldly announced that God has made all the events and relationships in life "beautiful," each having an appropriateness in and of themselves. And in addition to the beauty and appropriateness of this order of things, God has also implanted in the hearts of men a desire to know how his plan makes all the details fit together.

Everything, as it came from the hand of the Creator in Genesis 1, was "good" or "very good." Even the activities of verses 2-8, which in themselves do not always appear beautiful, have a beauty when they are seen as constituent parts of the whole work of God. In God's world plan, He "has made" all things to fit in their appointed time and place (v. 11). So integrated is this total work of God that man, likewise a creation of God, yearns in the depths of his being to trace the providential dealings of God's government from beginning to the end; yet he cannot.

The key word in 3:11 is "eternity" (*ha'olam*): "God has put *eternity* into their heart" (emphasis added).[7] This quest is a deep-seated desire, a compulsive drive, because people are made in the image of God and are made to appreciate the beauty of creation (on an aesthetic level); to know the character, composition, and meaning of the world (on an academic and philosophical level); and to discern its purpose and destiny (on a theological level). Therein lies the majesty and madness of the whole thing. Mortals

---

7    Brian P. Gault ("What Has God Placed in the Human Heart? An Analysis of Ecclesiastes 3:11," paper read at the *Evangelical Theological Society Meeting* on 15 November 2006) showed that there were no fewer than ten interpretive options for ha'olam, "eternity," utilizing metonymy, revocalization, and emendation to solve the problem. Sadly, he opts for "darkness" as the correct meaning, saying God desires people to stop trying to find the mysteries of His revealed will and to get on with living joyfully!

have an inborn inquisitiveness and capacity to learn how everything in their experience can be integrated to make a whole. They want to know how the mundane "downstairs" realm of ordinary, day-to-day living fits with the "upstairs" realm of the hereafter; how the business of living, eating, working, and enjoying can be made to fit with the call to worship, serve, and love the living God; and how one can accomplish the integration of the natural sciences, social sciences, and humanities. But in all the vastness and confusion of so much data, mortals are frustrated by the "puzzle" of selecting any one of the many facets of God's "good" world as that part of life to which they will totally give themselves instead of beginning with giving themselves totally to God first of all.

So, to state it plainly, one first has to come to terms with the living God. Life and its "goods" are gifts from the hands of the living God (vv. 13-15). Life will remain an enigma and a frustration until men and women come to "fear," that is, to believe, the God who made them, and that the goods, the truths, and all that is of this world is from our God. (See below for discussion of "the fear of God.") God's work and plan remain intact (v. 14). Just as men and women cannot, on their own, determine the end from the beginning of life, or one end from the other (v. 11), so also they cannot add anything to God's plan or take anything from it (v. 14).

Why then does God allow such a great burden of worries, or cares, frustrations, and labors to fall on one's shoulders if God can give: (1) mundane gifts, (2) the ability to enjoy those gifts, and (3) some knowledge of His all-encompassing plan? The answer is, "In order that they should fear before him" (v. 14). Obedience to the first commandment (Exod. 20:3) must come prior to receiving each of the above three requests; God must be Lord and Sovereign over all. Individuals must begin living by trusting nothing to their own abilities, devices, wisdom, or connections. "It is not," as Paul summarized in Romans 9:16, "to the one that wills [it], nor to one that runs, but to God who shows mercy."

The "fear of God" (3:14) appears in Ecclesiastes at several crucial points (see 5:7; 7:18; 8:12-13 [three times]; and 12:13). This "fear" is not an attitude of terror or dread. It is instead a commitment of the total being to trust and believe the living God. The preposition that accompanies the expression in 3:14 is forceful in supporting this view—"fear *before* him" (emphasis added; cf. 8:12). The absolute lordship of God in this expression is supported in the parallel invitation for all the nations to come and worship God and "fear before him," for "the Lord reigns" over the whole earth (cf. 1 Chron. 16:30; Psalm 96:9). The one who fears God dreads nothing more than God's disfavor. Such a worshiper wants nothing more than to know the living God intimately and submit to His will. And God Himself wants to be known and obeyed by mortals; accordingly, God has shut men and women up to the enigma of life, yet He has also given them an unquenchable hunger to know how it all fits, from the simplest to the most profound segment of life; everything must cohere and smoothly link with all of that which is around it.

God's purposes and His plan are unchangeable (v. 15). When the text says that God "calls back" or "seeks out" that which is "chased away," it refers either to those who are persecuted (as argued by Luther, Rashi, and the Midrash) or to time itself, which from a human point of view had been lost, but which in God's wise arrangement of events became available for God to be brought forward as a part of His wise plan, or as a witness at the last judgment. God, then, can in a sense call back the past and connect it with the future. With the hint of the divine evaluation in the future of the past deeds of men, we are prepared for the next section.

## B. 3:16–4:16 — The Facts: Anomalies Must Not Be Used By Us To Deny God's Plan

As noted already, six facts are brought forward by Solomon which otherwise might negate the thesis that God has a plan in operation that involves every person and every event.

[16]And something else I saw under the sun: in the place of justice, wickedness was there! And in the place of righteousness, injustice was there!

[17]I said in my heart: God will judge the righteous and the wicked, for there is a time for every matter and for every work.

[18]I said in my heart about the sons of the man, "God is testing them so that they can see that they are but animals.

[19]For what happens to the sons of the man is what happens to animals; one happening falls to both of them: as one dies so the other dies. All have one breath, man has no advantage [in that respect] over the animal, for everything is puzzling.

[20]All are going to one place: all came from the dust; all return to the dust.

[21]Who notices that the spirit of the sons of the man is the one going upwards and the spirit of the animals is the one going downwards to the earth?"

[22]So I saw that there was nothing better than a person should rejoice in one's work, for that is one's portion. For who will be able to bring one to see what will happen after him/her?

¹Again I turned and saw all the oppressions that are done under the sun, and oh the tears of the oppressed! For they had no one to comfort them. Power was in the hands of their oppressors, but they had no comforter.

²So I congratulated the dead who had already died more than the living who were still alive,

³but better still than both of them is the one who has not yet been, and has not seen the evil work that is done under the sun.

⁴I saw all the toil and all the success from work, but it is envied each by his neighbor. This is puzzling and a vexation of spirit.

⁵The fool folds his hand and eats his [own] flesh.

⁶Better is a handful with quietness than two hands full of toil and vexation of spirit.

⁷Again I turned and I saw a puzzle under the sun:

⁸There was one [man] without a second [one]; he had neither a son nor a brother; yet there was no end to all his toil. His eyes were not satisfied with wealth, "so for whom am I toiling and depriving myself of happiness [he said to himself]"? This too is a puzzling [business] and an unpleasant task.

⁹Two are better than one, because they have a good reward for their work.

¹⁰For if the one falls, the other can lift up his companion. But woe to the one who falls and there is no second person to help him up.

¹¹Also, if two lie down together, they keep warm. But how can you keep warm [alone]?

¹²Though one may be overpowered, two can stand against him [the enemy]; a three-ply cord is not quickly snapped.

[13]Better is a poor but wise child than an old and foolish king who does not know how to be admonished any longer.

[14]For from the prison house he emerged to reign; although he was born poor in his kingdom.

[15]I saw all the living, who were walking under the sun, along with the second child who would succeed him.

[16][There is] no end to all the people, to all who were before him; also the ones coming later will not rejoice in him. Even this also is a puzzle and a vexation of spirit.

## 1. Unrighteousness in the Halls of Government
### (3:16-17)

So grievous an exception to the overall plan of a good God is unrighteousness in the halls of government that Solomon immediately appended the words of verse 17 ("...God will judge righteousness and wickedness, for there is a time for every matter and for every work") as an answer to the charge of verse 16— "wickedness was in the place of justice." God had instituted human tribunals ("the place of judgment" [v. 16] is a court of law) as places where men could expect to find judicial relief. But when wickedness is offered where justice should be found, that is a matter of utmost seriousness. Similarly, "the place of righteousness" (v. 16) is the house of God, where one would also expect a fair hearing and correction of injustice and evil. Such inequities, when both the law courts and the house of God fail the oppressed, God Himself will rectify in the future judgment, even though their cases appear temporarily to run unattended and to be adjudicated unfairly. Wronging the innocent and clearing the guilty is dangerous business, for all who practice such crookedness and demagoguery will face the Judge of all judges in that final judgment.

Some have incorrectly argued that Qoheleth denied that there was any system of justice by which punishment would come to evildoers and God-fearing citizens would be protected. But such arguments asserting divine arbitrariness go counter to what the text clearly asserts. Verse 17 showed that the Teacher believed God would judge human beings even if the time when He did so was not always clearly stated—it is only the timing of God's judgment that is not declared here.

Moreover, what we know today as "activistic judges," who create their own new laws from the bench, without reference to any constitution or governing document, which new creations also usually run counter to God's laws, can expect God's judgment as well, even if it does not come until the future when all appear at the judgment seat of Christ.

## 2. Death Comes to All (3:18-21)

Although nothing is so prominent at times as the savage way men tyrannize one another in and out of the courts of the land, death ultimately catches up with all men. But there is the seeming unfairness of it all. Death is the great leveler of all living beings. It happens to men as it happens to beasts: both are subject to death.

Yet by this very same fact, God shows mortals their frailty in an effort to force them to turn back and search for Himself: to come to the realization that all goods are from His hand, to receive from His hand the ability to enjoy those gifts, and to come to appreciate His sovereign plan.

Tragically, we seldom take to heart as we ought to the reality of death. We moderns are more primitive in our estimate of and regard for the life hereafter than were the men of antiquity. We are insulated from directly facing the grim aspects of death day in and day out; it was not so with those in Solomon's day. They had no gadgetry to occupy their minds, no gracious living to cause them to forget, no hospitals and rest homes to remove the smell, sound, and sight of death or the death rattles from them.

Most people conclude that since "all go to one place" (v. 20), that is, the "grave" (here the idea is not "hell"), that is the end of it. Certainly, both men and beasts are made out of dust, and their bodies return to the dust; but what poor gamblers men and women are if they believe that that is the end of the matter. Verse 21 deliberately adds in the clearest tones possible (despite very little help from some translations or most commentators), "The spirit of man *goes upward*, but the spirit of the beast *goes down* to the earth" (emphasis mine). The verbs "to go upward" and "to go downward" are active participles with the article attached to them and not, as some incorrectly insist, the Hebrew sign of the interrogative. As Leupold has accurately rendered this concept, "There are not many who take to heart as they ought to the fact that the spirit of man goeth upward and that the spirit of the beast goeth downward to the earth."[8] The presence of the long "a" in the prefix *ha-* instead of the short "a" shows that the Hebrew scribes, called the Masoretes, did not regard verse 21 as an interrogative or conditional sentence. Had not Solomon also argued already that unjust judges will face the living God at some point (3:17)? And will not God with consistency press the same facts into service in Ecclesiastes 12:7: "The dust returns to the earth as it was, and the spirit returns to God who gave it"? What would be the point of concluding his book with the ominous warning about the future that "God

8    Leupold, *op. cit.*, p. 100.

will bring every deed into judgment" (12:14) if men and women are dead and gone forever once they die? If that were the case, who would care if God reprimanded our worms after we had long ceased to exist? Neither they nor our dust will much care. But such is not Solomon's thought.

Concepts of man's immortality are as old as Enoch, the seventh from Adam (Jude 14); his body entered the eternal state directly. Even patriarchal Job knew that death was not the end of life. He observed that if you chop down a tree, it often sends out new "shoots" from the old stump (Job 14:7). Likewise, he contested, if you chop down a man so that he dies, there is hope for him that he too will also "shoot" again in new life (Job 14:14; the same root word as in verse 7 is used here, although the fact is obscured in the translations). The same point of view was affirmed by the psalmist in Psalm 49:12-15, where he too argued that "man…is like the beasts that perish. Like sheep they are laid in the grave…But God will redeem my soul/life (Hebrew *nephesh*) from the power of the grave, for he will receive me", (NKJV).

If it is argued, as it often is, that verse 21 must be a question because it begins with "who knows," Leupold[9] convincingly protests that in the nine passages where this expression appears in the Hebrew Bible, only three are followed by the interrogative (Esther 4:14; Eccles. 2:19; 6:12). In another three cases, "Who knows" is followed by a direct object (Ps. 90:11; Eccles. 3:21; 8:1); three more times it is either followed by the imperfect verb, or it is a kind of afterthought and means something like "perhaps" (Prov. 24:24; Joel 2:14; Jonah 3:9). Only the context will determine whether or not the Hebrew phrase is interrogative. Here the phrase calls for

---

9    Leupold, *op. cit.*, p. 99.

a direct object and is not a nonchalant remark that no one is actually able to tell the difference between the fates of men and animals; they can and must!

Men and beasts, then, do differ. A person may be like the beasts in one way—his or her frail body may return to the dust. But his or her spirit/life goes upward to God; whether reserved for judgment or some more pleasant prospect, the writer does not pause at this point to say.

In the meantime, God has something that men may inherit: their portion, if they meet the previously stated conditions of belief, is that they may be able to enjoy their work in this life (v. 22). The rhetorical question "Who can bring him to appreciate what will be after him?" is again not answered at this point, but the context is abundantly clear, as is the conclusion to Ecclesiastes: it is God who will in the future evaluate life in its totality.

### 3. Oppression of God's People (4:1-3)

Another complaint emerges to threaten the beauty of the plan of God—oppression (4:1-3). What list of possible injuries that can be done to a person, their property, or a person's good name by rulers, masters, fathers, husbands, or any others in positions of power or responsibility, is found here? For those rulers have the power. The lot of the oppressed often is that there is the absence of any "comforter" (v. 1). To be without a comforter is worse than death itself (v. 2). Like Jonah (Jonah 4:3) and Elijah (1 Kings 19:4), the oppressed cry, "Lord, take away my life, for it is better for me to die than to live", (NIV). In fact, so powerfully wrong and so solitary does the case of the oppressed appear, that, like Job (Job 3:3-10), the oppressed prefer non-existence to existence (v. 3). Our mourner will not recover until he, like the psalmist Asaph (Ps. 73:17), goes into the house of

God (Eccles. 5:1-6) and considers what "the end" of such oppressors will be.

The problem of the oppressor and the oppressed in the history of mankind inevitably turned on the struggle of the strong over the weak; the strong who were able to impose their will over others. Even in a democracy there can be the "tyranny of the majority," if the principles guiding that majority are not taken from the Word of God. Without a God to answer to, humanists and secularists have little or no motivation to act righteously or to abstain from wickedness—especially if by that evil they can get their own way. As a result, the only outlook on life for such materialists is one of cynical resignation (vv. 2-3).

## 4. Envy from Others (4:4-6)

To the previous three obstacles to acceptance of the overall principle that God's plan encompasses everything is now added the observation that mortals can be as cruel and inhuman to each other in unnecessary competition as they can be in outright oppression. Often the rule of the business world is the law of the jungle. Every success is greeted with envy from others instead of the expected compliments or praise. "Every right work," or "every successful undertaking" (v. 4), is received as Cain greeted his brother Abel's goodness, or as Saul failed to rejoice over the success of David's undertakings against the enemy.

It might appear justifiable to just plain forget it all. Why should anyone want to work so hard in a dog-eat-dog world, only to be envied as the reward for one's success? Yet Qoheleth warns that such an attitude must not be an excuse for laziness. And to seal that logic, he adds a proverb (v. 5) against the idleness of the fool who folds his hands and comes to ruin, for he figuratively "eats his own flesh" as he consumes what substance he had stored up. In Proverbs 6:10 (also in 24:33), folded hands act as a symbol of idleness, which inevitably leads to poverty.

Instead of cruel competitiveness, Solomon recommends moderation. Verse 6 is similar to the Pauline injunction, "Godliness with contentment is great gain" (1 Tim. 6:6); or even the Solomonic proverbs: "Better is a little with the fear of the Lord" (Prov. 15:16, cf. v. 17; 17:1) and "Better is little with righteousness than great treasures with injustice" (Prov. 16:8). A small amount of food eaten in peace is to be preferred to an elaborate meal where strife is present as well.

## 5. Isolation and Solitariness (4:7-12)

There are more problems for theodicy, i.e., justifying the ways of God to mortals. What about the sadness of isolation and solitariness? Escape from competition may be a temporary solution, but then one has to cope with the issue of loneliness. This is a situation in which there is no family left, not even an heir for whom one could work and deprive one's self of pleasure. Previously we have seen "no comforter" (4:1-3) and "no rest" (4:4-6), but now there is "no companion" (4:7-12): What can be said to this situation?

Solomon had a proverb for this situation as well: "Two are better than one" (v. 9). Society, not the solitary life of a hermit or the like, and perhaps even marriage, but not the single life of celibacy, are to be preferred. For in such intimacy, and in the shared life, these are the resources that are made available: assistance (v. 10), comfort (v. 11), and defense of one another (v. 12). In each of the proverbs of verses 9-12, the advantages of cooperation and companionship are emphasized. In fact, if two are better than one, three friends provide even greater comradeship (v. 12b).

### 6. *Popularity is Temporary (4:13-16)*

With a slight variation in the order of things, the proverbial answer comes first this time (v. 13), whereas in this sixth, and final objection, the obstacle comes last. How fleeting and altogether temporary is the popularity accorded persons! What does it matter if someone has even royal power? In one case, the old king, although born to the throne, becomes foolish, senile, and unable to discern that his days of ruling are over. In another situation, a young (but poor and wise) person, like Joseph in the patriarchal times (see Gen. 37–50), may rise from prison to the throne. Such are the constant ups and downs of life, for although the young man was welcomed at first (v. 15), he, too, will no doubt share his predecessor's fate: "Those who come later will not be pleased with him" (v. 16). How fickle people are! Today's hero is tomorrow's bum. While rulers tremble and diligently seek to make their thrones secure, the people clamor for change and revolution. Now how can the plan of God encompass the likes of such disparities?

## C. 5:1-17 – The Implications: Certain Warnings and Cautions to Us Are in Order

Despite the reality of the obstacles just surveyed in 3:16–4:16, none of these can or should be offered as an excuse for neglecting one's relationship to God or for abandoning the concept that God's rule embraces all of reality. Even though some may be tempted to reflect on the six anomalies, or alleged contradictions, over against the universality of God's plan and purpose for everything and everyone, mortals must not be led into a practical atheism or be tempted to think or to act as if God were not in control.

(The numbering of the verses in chapter 5 differs in Hebrew from the English, for the last verse of chapter 4 in Hebrew is the first verse of chapter 5 in English, and so the numbering of the verses in Hebrew for the fifth chapter is always one less than the English verse number.)

[1](4:17H) Guard your steps when you go into the house of God; draw near to listen rather than to offer the sacrifice of fools, for they do not know that they do evil.

[2](1H) Do not be rash with your mouth, and do not let your heart be hasty to utter anything before God, for God is in heaven and you are on the earth, therefore let your words be few.

[3](2H) As a dream comes when there are many activities, so a fool's speech is accompanied by many words.

[4](3H) When you make a vow to God, do not delay in fulfilling it; for he has no pleasure in fools. Pay what you have vowed.

[5](4H) It is better not to vow than that you should make a solemn promise and not pay it.

[6](5H) Do not let your mouth cause you to sin. And do not say before the messenger, "It was a mistake!" Why should God be furious with what you say and destroy the work of your hands?

[7](6H) For many dreams and many words are worthless; instead, fear God.

[8](7H) If you see the poor oppressed and robbery of justice and rights throughout the district, do not be astonished at such matters, for one official is watching another official and over both of them are others higher still.

⁹(8H) And an advantage of the land in everything is this: a king benefits from a field.

¹⁰(9H) Whoever loves silver [money] will not be satisfied with silver [money]. Whoever loves wealth will not profit; this too is a puzzle.

¹¹(10H) As goods increase, those consuming them increase. What is the advantage to their owners, except that their eyes look on them?

¹²(11H) The sleep of the laborer is sweet, whether he eats a little or much; but the abundance of the rich does not allow him to sleep.

¹³(12H) There is a serious evil I have seen under the sun; riches were hoarded by their owner to his harm.

¹⁴(13H) But that wealth was lost to a bad venture, so that when he fathered a son, there was nothing left for him.

¹⁵(14H) As he came out from his mother's womb, naked shall he depart, just as he came, and he will carry nothing from his labor which he can take in his hand.

¹⁶(15H) This too is a serious evil, exactly as he came, so he will go. What profit does he have for all that he labors for the wind?

¹⁷(16H) All his days he eats in darkness with much vexation, sickness and frustration.

The Teacher's strong advice for us, above all else, is to "go to the house of God" (5:1), but we are to go with a receptive attitude and a readiness to listen rather than lecture God on what He ought to do or how things should be run. Worship is here called "sacrifice" because it is offering to God "the calves/fruit of our lips" (the Hebrew word for both terms is very similar; cf. Hosea 14:2; Heb. 13:15) in lieu of animal sacrifices. The implication seems to be that the "sacrifice of fools" consists of excessive talk, especially talk that has little or no heart behind it, which seems to be borne out in verse 2. Therefore, to avoid looking like a fool, it is best to limit one's speaking in God's presence and be more ready to listen to what God has to say instead of offering a lot of chatter. Do not give the impression from your blustering verbiage that you believe you have achieved some kind of super status and what you have to say is all that important—to God (or even to human beings). Remember, you are on earth and God is in heaven!

Neither should men attempt to bribe God with vows (vv. 4-7). How frivolous and unbecoming can mere mortals act? "God is in heaven and [we] are on earth" (5:2), as Solomon had already reminded us. Therefore, our words should be few. And thereby we are rebuked for all pretense, hypocrisy, and superficial religiosity by which we hope to be heard merely for our verbosity or "much speaking" (cf. Matt. 6:7). Limits are imposed only on the petitioner's pretense, and not on the length of his prayers. There may be times when a person's importunity (and hence the length and persistence of one's prayer) demonstrates the value and importance of what one asks from God, by the fact that the request is serious enough to be persistently on one's mind, even as Jacob refused to let the Angel of the Lord go until he blessed him (Gen. 32:26). On the other hand, only fools babble on relentlessly, like a man who has had a busy day and experiences dream after dream all night long (v. 3).

But when vows are made to God, they must be carried out (v. 5). Ananias and Sapphira deliberately lied, when there was no need for them to do so, and therefore they experienced the serious judgment of God (Acts 5:1-11). It would have been better had they never vowed anything at all, or even if they had promised to give to God only a part of their land, rather than pretending that they too were giving the proceeds for the entire parcel to the apostles; but they had decided to toy with God in the hopes of gaining greater esteem in the estimation of the other believers in the early church.

The application of verses 6-7 is clear: do not sin with your mouth and do not protest to God's minister (the Hebrew word literally meaning "angel"; cf. Hag. 1:13 and Mal. 2:7, where "angel" means "priest," or "minister," for the Lord. The Greek Septuagint translated the Hebrew word for "messenger" or "angel" as "God," perhaps as the "Angel of the Lord"?). Accordingly, we must watch our mouths when we contemplate such obstacles to faith and enigmas as life produces (cf. Matt. 5:33-36). Men must learn that their first order of business is to fear God. True piety is the only remedy for every temptation offered us to spew out a sally of empty words against God's good operation of all things. This conclusion agrees with 12:13. A mortal must begin as a believer and worshiper if he is ever to enjoy living as God intended him to live.

Now that Solomon has established his dominant theme—the fear of God as his (and our) number-one priority (v. 7)—he now turns to some of the cases he had previously introduced. His work moves more and more in the direction of a theodicy, that is, an explanation and justification of the ways of God to men. Commentators typically disallow this type of "fear of God" to be connected with anything like a "reverential awe of God," or leading to any emotional and sacred attachment to God Himself. They refuse to connect this verse with 12:13, claiming that the so-called "frame-narrator" in 12:13 meant a higher meaning than what Qoheleth meant here in verse 7. But that analysis is one that is foisted on the text rather than one that comes directly from the text itself.

The Teacher moves from advising what our relationship should be to God in verses 1-7 to noting how we should relate to the king in verses 8-17 and how our wealth and possessions are to be shared with both.

First of all, in the problem of the perversion of justice (see 3:16-18), Qoheleth now appeals in 5:8 to the fact that there remains a tribunal that is higher than those officials who perpetrate those wrongs. It is the tribunal owned and operated by God. Some have choked on the word "province" or "district" (v. 8, Hebrew *medinah*) and argued that the word was unknown in Israel during Solomon's time, as it must be a Persian loan-word in their judgment. But it must be remembered that Solomon was acquainted with many languages because of his many contacts with the nations of the world. Thus it is natural that he would use a word for a "district" found outside of Israel in Persia at that time. Nevertheless, however we evaluate the word "district," let no one be surprised, the highest judge of all is the One who will evaluate every judgment ever made in any court of law—then or now!

Verse 9 continues in the same vein of thought. Good government by a delegated officer, or the "higher-up" person, is a great blessing to any country. This is one source of correction of some of the abuses witnessed by mortals. Happy indeed is that country that recognizes that such "profit" of the land brings a blessing on everyone; ruler and people are happiest when they both realize that they are served by the farmed fields. But should human government also fail, there is still redress from God, who will not fail to adjudicate the injustices and unfair acts of those who govern.

As for the other problems previously raised, Solomon summarizes his case in 5:10-17. It is a case for the unsatisfactory nature of wealth and labor in and of themselves. There is little, if any, "benefit" in riches *per se*, he says. Consider that:

- Human desire outruns acquisitions, no matter how large the acquisitions may be (v. 10).

- An increase in wealth demands a corresponding increase in staff to manage it. Wealth, unfortunately, seems to attract all sorts of parasites (v. 11).

- Labor may bring sleep, but wealth brings sleeplessness and the fear that a blunder may result in the loss of everything (v. 12).

- Possession is so uncertain and so brief, for often by some accident or speculation (evil travail or misfortune, v. 14) the estate dwindles down to nothing.

- Last of all, the wealthy person himself must return to his or her Maker devoid of all the riches, not even having a cloak (vv. 13-16). Nevertheless, there still are people who will spend all their days in great sorrow and distressing labor for such an empty goal as this (v. 17).

### D. 5:18-20 — Conclusion

The conclusion remains the same as we have noted above (5:18-20, Hebrew, vv. 17-19): man must get enjoyment, not possessions, out of life. And that capacity to enjoy them, no matter how great or how small, must come as a gift from God. It is much better to receive wealth as a gift from God, simultaneously with the God-given ability to enjoy it, than to see wealth and riches as ends in themselves. The condition for the reception of this gift is the same as it was in 2:26, and therefore it is not repeated.

How sad that mortals spend all their days working and sweating to receive the enjoyment that God offers as a gift if people would only seek it in the manner that He, in his excellent and beautiful plan, has chosen to give it. Happiness, enjoyment, pleasure, and a knowledge of how the whole substance of life is integrated into a meaningful pattern in the plan of God are all linked in the living God. To know the "eternity" of all things, if we may rephrase John 17:3, is "to know Him."

# 3

# EXPLAINING AND APPLYING THE PLAN OF GOD

## *Ecclesiastes 6:1–8:15*

Qoheleth, the "Teacher," has shown so far that any and all enjoyment in life must come as a gift from God. This gift of enjoyment from God is preferable, for example, to accumulating ever so much wealth and so many possessions apart from knowing God. Moreover, all the events of life and the persons on earth are regulated by a beautiful plan which also comes from God. These two conclusions from the first two sections of our work prepare us for section three, Ecclesiastes 6:1–8:15, which is the central portion of the whole argument of Solomon's book.

Here, Qoheleth will apply the two conclusions gained thus far in this book (concerning the gifts and plan of God) to a list of common objections to such a thesis as the overruling providence of God. He will entertain questions about inequalities and instances of injustice that are found in life.

This third section, then, consists of three subsections and a conclusion:

A. 6:1–7:15—A Proper Evaluation of Our *Outward* Fortunes Will Help to Explain the Apparent Inequalities in Divine Providence

B. 7:16-29—A Proper Evaluation of Our Inner *Character* Will Help to Explain the Apparent Inequalities in Divine Providence

C. 8:1-14—The Removal of a Large Proportion of the Apparent Inequalities in Divine Providence Comes From *Righteous Government*

D. 8:15—Conclusion

Consistent with our approach thus far in this commentary, we will begin this central section in his argument by examining Solomon's conclusion to see where he thought he came out. To follow the argument of each part, we must have some idea of where it was that the writer thought his evidence was leading him. That conclusion can be found at the end of this section, in Ecclesiastes 8:15, where once again the formula we have seen twice before (2:24-26; 5:18-20, which also appears in a partial conclusion in 3:22) reappears here as a colophon as it did in the two preceding sections of Ecclesiastes. However, the formula adds something to this repeated set of lines, which goes way beyond the so-called Epicurean "eat, drink and be merry, for tomorrow we die" formula, as both colophons previously did. Instead, it once again differ from the so-called Epicurean formulas as it reads this time:

> [15]So I commended joy, because there is nothing better for a person under the sun than to eat, drink and rejoice; for it will accompany him in his toil all the days of his life that God gives him under the sun.

The word *hassimchah* is rendered "the joy" [of life], as in 2:1, since Qoheleth is not commending "mirth," or sheer "pleasure," in any hedonistic fashion or for its own merits, but in keeping with the theme of the book, a "joy" that comes as a gift from God, which is the joy that Solomon is seeking.[1] All too many have inferred that to "eat, drink, and be merry" was an invitation to become drunk and to eat in an overindulgent manner. But there is no necessary reason why this must be the correct way to understand this word in this context.

For example, when the Book of the Law was read in Nehemiah's day, Nehemiah told the Israelites to "Go and enjoy food and sweet drinks" (Neh. 8:10), for that day was to be "holy to the Lord." Then all the people did just that: they ate, drank and shared portions with each other and they celebrated with "great joy" (Hebrew *simchah gedolah*; Neh. 8:12).[2] This joy (*chedvat*, a synonym for "joy" this time) from the Lord was [to be] their strength (Neh. 8:10, *ki chedvat YHWH hi' ma'uzzekem*).

God was to be praised for giving one of His most excellent gifts to the men and women who feared Him, the gift of "joy." This gift of the joy of living in the favor of God, "*will* remain/accompany" (not "*should* remain," as some render it, for it is a Hebrew indicative and not a Hebrew jussive form of the verb) "in his work all the days of the life God has given him under the sun", (NIV). God's gifts are not dangled on a string, as it were, before

---

1    That is how Whybray also rendered it, "So I praise joy." R. N. Whybray, "Qoheleth, Preacher of Joy," *Journal for the Study of the Old Testament* 23 (1982): 87.

2    A parallel text suggested to me by Glenn Fobert in an unpublished manuscript, p. 101.

the eyes of mortals, only to be retracted just as they seem to come in reach of them. God's promise is that, in His good plan, this gift of joy will accompany those who trust the Lord.

God's intention, then, was that mortals were to come to a proper joy in the material gifts placed in this world by God Himself. This joy was to be a source of constant satisfaction to men and women when these things and their users were properly aligned with their Giver. Moreover, it was meant that this joy would be part of the joy mortals would experience all the days of their lives.

Instead of all the restless activity of mortals, solely devoted to accumulating things and often using unjust and evil ways to obtain them, God has given a confident contentment as part of that joy that supersedes what otherwise would turn out to be indulging in a wicked hoarding of possessions and riches. Therefore, no person who truly fears God need ever stoop to any sort of low means to obtain what God has not yet gifted to them. Why trade a life of emptiness that is full of transitions and change for the contentment that can come from rejoicing in what comes from the hands of our Creator and Redeemer in His timing and in His plan?

## A. 6:1-7:15 — A Proper Evaluation of Our *Outward* Fortunes Will Help to Explain the Apparent Inequalities in Divine Providence

Two subdivisions carry out Solomon's argument as he looks at these external or outward circumstances. They are:

1. Prosperity is not Always or Necessarily a Good— 6:1-12

2. Adversity or Affliction is not Always or Necessarily an Evil—7:1-15

Let us see how each argument is developed so that we can come to a proper estimate of the fairness and goodness that is to be found in the plan of God. We shall look first at the outward array of realities that seem to be possible roadblocks to receiving the joy of the Lord in life.

## *1. Prosperity is Not Always or Necessarily a Good (6:1-12)*

[1]There is an adversity that I have seen under the sun, and it is great/heavy on a person.

[2]A person to whom God gives riches, possessions, and honor, so he lacked nothing of all he craved, but God did not empower him to enjoy any of it, for a stranger devoured it [instead]; this is a puzzle; it is a grievous sickness.

[3]If a man begets a hundred children and lives many years—and [if] the days of his years are many—but his soul is not filled with goodness, and he does not have a [proper] burial, I say, "Better is stillborn child than he."

[4]For into a transitory [world] he came and in the darkness he went, and in the darkness his name is covered.

[5]Although it has never seen the sun or known anything, this one has more rest than that one,

[6]even if he lives a thousand years twice over, but does not see good—do not both go to the one place?

[7]All a person's effort is for his mouth, yet his appetite is never filled.

[8]For what advantage has a wise person over a fool? What does a poor person have who knows [how] to walk [i.e., conduct himself] before the living?

[9]Better is the sight of the eyes than the wandering of the appetite. Here too is a puzzle and a vexation of spirit.

[10]Whatever happens, already his name has been called, and what a person is, is known; he is not able to contend with one stronger than he.

[11]For with many words, the puzzle increases; what advantage does a person have?

[12]Who knows what is good for a person in [this] life, from the number of days of his puzzling life he passes as a shadow? Who can tell a person what will happen after him under the sun?

Commentators all too frequently judge that the basic theme of this section is the lack of satisfaction mortals receive from their work. This, they complain, is in direct contrast with the *carpe diem* ["seize the day"] of Ecclesiastes 5:18-20. But this is to misjudge the structure of this book and to read it all too atomistically, as if these words were all separated aphorisms or proverbs that were randomly connected.

Instead, each of the statements listed here is used purposefully to lead one to the conclusion that the Teacher himself came to under the inspiration of God: "Never judge a book by its cover," as another old proverb says. Mortals should never get confused about the true state of others' affairs by looking merely at their outward state of affairs. A person may possess wealth, honor, numerous children, long life, and virtually every outward good that anyone could possibly imagine; yet he can still be a very broken, dissatisfied, and unhappy person. This is because God has deliberately isolated the gift of the goods themselves from the gift of the power to be able to enjoy those same gifts!

In 5:19 God had given to some both the possessions *and* the power to enjoy those possessions. In this instance, God has held back the power to enjoy wealth, possessions, and honor. But why has God chosen to act one way in one case and another way in a different case? That is not revealed to us here. In both situations, however, the Lord remains sovereign and has a purpose He is working out for each individual.

Perhaps this is why this is a weight that weighs heavily on men (6:1): God may grant a person wealth, possessions, honor, and virtually anything any heart desires, yet He does this without also granting that person the ability to enjoy any of it (6:2) in one case, while also granting that power to enjoy those things in another! Therein lies the point made by Solomon: things are not always what they seem to be. Prosperity, itself a gift, is in itself unfulfilling until God also gives the divine gift of the power to enjoy it. In fact, God-given wealth without the *God-given power to enjoy it* is a major malady. Worst of all is the fact that a stranger, not even his own kin, may consume the whole estate, from which a man had only joylessly partaken portions, yet without any evidence of a gift-given ability to enjoy it. At the very least, "This is puzzling" (*hebel*).

So immense is this deprivation of enjoyment that even if the case just mentioned were reversed and, instead of his being childless and leaving his possessions to a total stranger, that same man were instead blessed with an abundance of children (6:3; a "hundred children"—a typical oriental hyperbole illustrating a conscious exaggeration); and if, instead of departing from this earthly scene quickly and letting a stranger receive a bonanza of goods, he lived for an unusually long number of days (say, two thousand years, 6:6;—another hyperbole); still, if he were not given the divine gift of enjoying it all, death at birth would have been preferable to what had happened to such an individual (6:3). A stillborn baby is free from all the suffering of the joylessly rich person and has "more rest" than that one does (6:4-5). All this is true despite the typical examples of divine blessing, which are a large progeny and a long life (Gen. 25:8; 35:9-11; Job 42:17). But the possession of the good, in these cases, cannot offset the best when these same good gifts come with the power to enjoy them in God's good providence and gifting.

Again, in the concessions made in verses 3-5, we see that even if an inordinate number of days were offered to this man, those days must come to an end sometime up ahead. Then he too must go to the same place as the stillborn child (6:6). That "one place," as seen in 3:20, is the "grave." What then? If even the longest life eventually terminates without having yielded any enjoyment, not to mention any prospect of anything to follow for those who do not fear God, what is the benefit, or advantage, of all those years? Although others may have looked on with envious eyes, the truth is that the extension of days was not what it appeared to be; it only compounded that individual's sorrow.

Normally a long life is God's reward for living in a way that is pleasing to Him (cf. Exod. 20:12), but if in that long life there is no joy or satisfaction, what benefit would living long offer? The gift of enjoyment, once again, must come from God, for it cannot be found anywhere else.

Whereas a person's labor was continually aimed at one's insatiable desire for gratification ("his mouth"); nevertheless, many seem never able to arrive at their goal (6:7). No mortal, be they wise, poor, or rich, can satisfy their desires on their own (6:8). True, making do with what we possess is better than striving for what we do not have, for all the wishing in the world for things we want is worthless (6:9) if God has not given them as a gift. Similar to our proverb that "Better is a bird in the hand than two in the bush," so verse 9 urges us to enjoy what we have, even though we might be poor, for being satisfied with what we see and presently have is better than continually desiring what is imaginary and unrealistic.

Repeatedly the reason given why riches fail to yield any happiness continues to rest on the unalterable ordinance of God (6:10). Mortals, the creation of God, cannot set aside or overcome that divinely established connection between earthly things and the otherwise rampant dissatisfaction with those things apart from knowing and receiving by faith these gifts from the hand of God. Try as an individual may to wrestle with and contest God's decision to link these things and to make them one's own on one's own abilities and strength, it still is useless. The more a person talks, the more vapid, empty, and unsatisfactory the situation becomes (6:11). All words are useless and just so much hot air; a person might just as well acknowledge one's own limitations and begin immediately to start fearing God as the proper starting point. The ordinance of God dictates the incapacity of worldly things to yield their enjoyment on their own; in fact, it must be observed that often worldly prosperity, *by itself*, only increases the emptiness and dissatisfaction. We might ask, in the words of Paul in Romans 9:20, "Who art thou, O man, to talk back to God?" Do you know "what is good for man?" (6:12). Does *anyone* know what the future holds? Of course, no one knows except God. Therefore, no one can say what will be the real advantage of one thing or another, either for one's self or for others. It is not as if Solomon finally throws up his hands in the air and concludes in despair, "no one knows what is good for mortals to do or what will happen in the future." But verse 10 makes it clear that God surely knows both what is good for mortals and what is in the future.

If every one of the above cases has shown the inadequacy of judging the fairness and goodness of the plan of God by observing merely the external features, then the providence of God may not have so many exceptions as we may have thought as we began to apply the truth of 3:1—that there is a time and season for everything under heaven—especially when compared to the apparent success of the wicked. Prosperity may not always be what it seems. Therefore, let us seek to know God, to be content with such gifts as He gives us, and to receive the accompanying gift of enjoyment from His hands.

## 2. Adversity or Affliction is Not Always or Necessarily an Evil (7:1-15)

The companion truth to 6:1-12 is now set forth in 7:1-15—suffering and adversity are not the inevitable or necessary signs of God's disfavor. In fact, adversity may often be a greater good than evidences of prosperity.

> ¹Better is a good name than fine ointment, and the day of death than the day of one's birth.
>
> ²Better to go to the house of mourning than to go into the house of feasting: for that is the end of every person, and the living should take it to heart.
>
> ³Better is sorrow than laughter, for with the sadness of the face the heart is made well.
>
> ⁴The heart of the wise is in the house of mourning, but the heart of fools is in the house of gaiety.

⁵Better to hear the rebuke of the wise, than to listen to the song of fools.

⁶For as the sound of thorns [crackling] under the pot, so is the laughter of fools; This too is a puzzle.

⁷Oppression makes a wise person look foolish, and a bribe corrupts the heart.

⁸Better is the end of a matter than its beginning; better is a patient spirit than a haughty one.

⁹Do not be hasty in your spirit to take offense, for resentment lodges in the bosom of fools.

¹⁰Do not say, "How was it that the former days were better than these?" For it is not from wisdom that you ask this.

¹¹Wisdom is good with an inheritance, and an advantage to those seeing the sun.

¹²Surely, wisdom is a shelter as silver [money] is a shelter. And the advantage of knowledge is that wisdom gives life to those possessing it.

¹³Consider the work of God: who is able to straighten what he made crooked?

¹⁴In the day of prosperity be happy, and in the day of adversity, consider; God has set the one alongside the other, so that no one will find out what will be after him.

¹⁵Everything I have seen in the days of my puzzlement: there is a righteous one who perishes in his righteousness and there is a wicked one who prolongs his wickedness.

The question has already been posed in 6:12, "What is good?" This becomes the hook on which a series of proverbs, giving us some "good" or "better" things, are hung. Here are some "good" or "better" things that will prove to be more salutary than prosperity:

- A good name is better than expensive perfume (7:1a). This may well refer to the practice in Biblical times of anointing a dead body with spices and perfume to make the corpse more presentable, but Solomon's retort is that it is more preferable to have a good reputation ("name") than a sweet-smelling body on one's deathbed.

- The day of death is better than the day of birth, with its promise of prosperity (7:1b). Life, advised Solomon, is often filled with vexing events, even though it is possible for one with a good reputation to be praised for a life well-lived.

- Mourning is better than festivity and mirth (7:2). Funerals are not as much fun as a birthday party, but we mortals do much more sober thinking at a funeral than we do at some festive celebrations.

- Sorrow is better than laughter (7:3). While often laughter is good for the soul, yet a sad face may open up the heart more than the hollow ring of robust joviality. Some are not even capable of facing death (7:4), for they flee from death and try to drown any thoughts about it with alcohol and anything else except sober reflection.

- Rebuke from a wise person is better than the praise of fools (7:5). This is true for all times and situations rather than just times of avoiding going to funerals.

- Thorn bush fires flare up quickly into a huge fire, but they also just as quickly die down and are therefore short-lived. The sound of "fools' laughter" is much like the Hebrew assonance (a literary technique using words that sound alike) of "nettles" under the "kettles"—(*hassirim*, "the thorns", under the *hassir*, "the kettle"; note the "song of fools" (*shir kesilim*, in 7:5)—their laughter is just that stupid sounding and short lived!

- "Oppression" (v. 7, cf. 4:1), not "extortion" as the NIV and some translate it, often turns wise persons into looking and acting like fools. Likewise "bribes," along with "oppression," put a lot of pressure on a person to do what they would not do ordinarily. The attack, in any case, is on the person's heart. They become brainwashed and their views distorted from the standard found in the character of God.

- The end of a thing is better than its beginning (7:8). Otherwise, we procrastinate and put matters off that could have been carried out in much better form had we not delayed working on them.

- "Patience" (7:8b) in waiting for God's timing is better than fretting over the elusiveness of things (7:8-9). It may be that the impatient are those who have a haughty spirit and who try to fix things by using force or yelling at others. Persons who are quick to get angry (7:9) are those who carry over anger from other situations and often are unwilling to work through a problem before blowing up over it.

- Further affliction may be better than any immediate outward good (7:10-12). Often the "good old days" were not as good as we seem to remember them. Therefore, wishing for the past to return is living in the past instead of living in the present. It is more advantageous to take shelter in wisdom, for wisdom, like money, can protect us from some of the hardships on earth.

Thus the scenes of sadness in 7:1-6 set the stage for the argument of this section. Present grief and pain may prove to be more beneficial in their effect on us than all the festivity, mirth, and jovial laughter of the outwardly prosperous and successful person. Solomon makes his point with various proverbs and with Hebrew words of similar sound (a figure of speech called *paronomasia*). For example, this occurs in verse 1 ("name," in Hebrew pronounced *shem,* and "perfume," Hebrew *shemen)* and, as we pointed out above, in verses 5 and 6 ("song," Hebrew *shir;* "pot," Hebrew *sir;* "thorns," Hebrew *sirim,* or as we say in English, "As the noise of *nettles* under the *kettle[s]*").

In verse 1, Solomon points to those things that are more abiding than the rich man's mirth. A good reputation ("name") has an influence (like the aroma of the perfume) beyond its owner's own lifetime. The day of a man's death also has a lasting influence, for afterward his life can be held forth as an example if his name has merited it.

The second proverb, in verse 2, is not much different from what our Lord said in the Sermon on the Mount: "Blessed are they that mourn" (Matt. 5:4). There is a mellowing that takes place in affliction and sorrow in some, while in others it tends to harden them and make them more bitter. To be in the presence of sickness or death has a tendency to bring us quickly to the really crucial issues of life.

Likewise the third proverb, in verses 3-4, teaches that there is a lesson to be gained from, and a work to be accomplished by, sorrow in the lives of those who fear God.

Contrariwise, the prattle, hilarity, and laughter of fools (vv. 5-6) are basically useless, hollow, and bothersome in and of themselves. We, with David, should much more prefer the kind smiting and rebuke that comes from the righteous (Ps. 141:5) to the profitless joviality that does not build up the soul.

When the head of a ruler or judge is turned by rewards in exchange for his oppression of someone's enemy (as for example, through an unfair rendering of justice), we can be sure that such a bribe will "destroy the heart"; that is, it will corrupt one's understanding and blind the judge's sense of justice and values (7:7) to the hurt of those who expect better from the judge.

In all cases, it is better to wait for God's timing than to be impatient (7:8-9). To worry unnecessarily or prematurely is to give way to a fool's approach to problems. Neither must we wish for the good old days, with their real or imaginary advantages and pleasures in comparison to the present situation (7:10). Surely, true wisdom would view things differently (7:11-12). Of such wisdom Solomon wrote in Proverbs: "Whoever finds me, finds life" (Prov. 8:35); and "The fear of the Lord, this is wisdom" (Prov. 1:7; 9:10; see also Job 28:28).

The truth of the matter is that affliction is from the appointment of God (7:13-14). The "crooked" that needed straightening (v. 13; cf. 1:15) is perhaps found in the presence of afflictions and adversities in life. No wonder the text exclaims (to paraphrase the point):

> Look with wonder, admire, and silently wait for the result of God's work! The contrasts of life are deliberately allowed by God so that men should ultimately develop a simple trust and dependence on God.
>
> For prosperity and the goods from God's hand, be thankful and rejoice. But in adversity and the crookedness of life, think. Reflect on the goodness of God and the comprehensiveness of His plan for men.

Therefore, although men appear to be treated irrespective of their character in the providence of God (7:15), the just man perishing in his righteousness and the evil man apparently prolonging his life in his wickedness, this is again only "judging a book by its cover," or using external appearances by which to judge the whole case. Such a verdict is premature and improperly grounded. We must penetrate more deeply beneath the surface if we are to properly evaluate either of these men or the plan and ordinance of God.

## B. 7:16–8:1 — A Proper Evaluation of Our Inner *Character* Will Help to Explain the Apparent Inequalities in Divine Providence

Solomon has warned us that if we are to properly reconcile the ways of God with the disappointments of men, we must avoid judging persons and events by mere outward impressions or appearances, whether it results from prosperity (6:1-12) or adversity and affliction (7:1-15). A second consideration is now introduced: those whom we suppose to be experiencing unfair suffering may not be as good as we suppose them to be.

[16]Do not multiply [your] righteousness, neither think yourself overly furnished with wisdom—why destroy yourself?

[17]Do not multiply [your] wickedness and do not be a fool—why die before your time?

[18]It is good to take hold of this [one of the extremes mentioned in the two previous verses] and also not to let go of the other. For the one who fears God will come forth with all of them.

[19]Wisdom strengthens the wise more than ten rulers who are in the city,

²⁰because there is not a righteous man on earth who does what is right and never sins.

²¹Also, do not take to heart every word people say lest you hear your servant cursing you.

²²For you also know that many times in your heart you yourself have declared others accursed.

²³All this I tested by wisdom: I said, "I will be wise," but it was far from me.

²⁴That which is, is far off, and unfathomable, very unfathomable. Who can discover it?

²⁵I myself turned my mind to understand, to explore, and to seek wisdom and a reckoning [of things], and to understand the wickedness of stupidity and the folly of foolishness.

²⁶I find more bitter than death the woman whose heart is snares and nets, and whose hands are fetters; the one pleasing God will flee to safety from her, but the one sinning will be captured by her.

²⁷"Look, this is what I have discovered," says the Teacher, "[Adding] one thing to another to find the conclusion—

²⁸(which my soul still seeks, but I have not found), one man among a thousand I found, but a woman among all of these I have not found."

²⁹See, this only I found: that God made man upright, but they—they have gone in search of many schemes.

¹Who is like the wise man and who knows the interpretation of things? Wisdom lightens up the face of a man and [the] harshness of his face is changed.

Few verses in Ecclesiastes are more susceptible to incorrect interpretations than 7:16-18. For many, Solomon's advice is the so-called "golden mean"; it is as if he had said: "Don't be too holy and don't be too wicked—sin only to a moderate degree!" What such commentators believe Qoheleth is teaching is that there is a sort of "golden mean" between virtue and vice. But this conclusion also dates the book late, since the idea of a "mean" that guides one's life only gained prominence during Aristotle's day or that of the Stoics. Such a "middle way" was advocated by the Eastern religions, such as Buddhism,[3] but it is not at home in Scripture.

What such commentators miss is that verses 16-17 are not cautioning against possessing too much real righteousness. The danger is that mortals might delude themselves and others through a multiplicity of pseudo-religious acts of sanctimoniousness or ostentatious showmanship in the act of worship: in some, a spirit of hypercriticism against minor deviations from one's own cultural norms, which are equated with God's righteousness, and in others, a disgusting conceit and supercilious, holier-than-thou attitude veneered over the whole mess.

Wayne Brindle disagreed, for he felt 7:16-17 warned against an overreaction to the statement in 7:15 that righteousness does not guarantee prosperity nor wickedness death. Instead of following the views Whybray and Castellino and I have set forth, that verses 16-17 begin a new section and the statements about being "excessively righteous" and "overly wise" are warnings against self-righteousness and pretended wisdom, Brindle sees these expressions only as seeking after perfection and

3    See Robert Gordis, *Koheleth—The Man and His World*, 3rd ed. (New York: Schocken, 1968, pp. 178, 276) and Harold H. Watts, *The Modern Reader's Guide to Religions* (New York: 1964, p. 540).

super-wisdom.[4] But Brindle has not successfully tied in his understanding of the passage with verse 18 as follows in our discussion.

The real clue to this passage, as George R. Castellino demonstrated, is that the second verb in verse 16, "to be wise," must be rendered reflexively (for it is the Hebrew *Hithpael* form) as "to think oneself to be furnished with wisdom." Furthermore, Castellino observed, even if this valid point about the reflexive nature of the verb is rejected for some reason, "Do not be wise" in verse 16 is to be understood as it is in Proverbs 3:7: "Be not wise *in your own eyes*" (ESV, emphasis added).[5] Accordingly, verse 17 would follow the same pattern as established for verse 16, because the two verses are part of the same thought. The resulting translation for verses 16-17 is:

> [16]Do not multiply [your] righteousness and do not play the part of the wise [in your own eyes; see Prov. 3:7]—why destroy yourself?

> [17]Do not multiply [your] wickedness and do not be a [downright] fool—why die before your time?

The correctness of this interpretation can be demonstrated by its compatibility with verse 18. It is good, says Solomon, that men should take hold of "this," namely, true wisdom that comes from the fear of God, rather than grasping "that," namely, the folly of fools. It is the fear of God that is the best

---

4    Wayne A. Brindle, "Righteousness and Wickedness in Ecclesiastes 7:15-18," *Andrews University Seminary Studies* 23 (1985): 243-57.

5    George R. Castellino, "Qohelet and His Wisdom," *Catholic Biblical Quarterly* 30 (1968): 24. See also R. N. Whybray, "Qoheleth the Immoralist? (Qoh. 7:16-17)," in *Israelite Wisdom: Theological and Literary Essays in Honor of Samuel Terrien*, ed. John G. Gammie (Missoula, MT: Scholars, 1978), pp. 191-204.

protection against either absurdity. Neither man's folly nor a conceited and strained righteousness will serve as a guide, or as a guise, to mask the real need of men. They must come to fear God. That is true wisdom. Wisdom, then, is not a self-imposed estimate of one's own abilities or attainments. Indeed, true wisdom will be a better protection against all these errors and excesses than ten rulers or sultans in a city (v. 19).

We cannot be too careful in our evaluation of the character of men. Too much passes for true piety that is not piety at all. The only thing a pseudo-pious kind of scrupulosity will yield is the judgment of God. Therefore, warns Qoheleth, the Teacher, let us not be too quick to label the providence of God as unjust.

In fact, rather than being too pious, no one is without fault in deed or word (vv. 20-22). Men are universally depraved, and we all fall short of the glory of God. The advantage (v. 20 begins with a "because") of the recommended wisdom in fearing God (v. 18) is that it does more than open up the pattern of meaning to the eternity of all things here below and above (3:11); this wisdom also gives men and women a self-control that will not resent the ill-advised slander, abuse, and curses of others. It is foolish to be overly concerned about and troubled by what others think and say about us in their unguarded, unkind, and foolish moments (vv. 21-22).

Nevertheless, it still must be said of even the wisest of us that despite the original uprightness of man as he came from the hand of his Maker in the Garden of Eden, we have one and all alike gone after our own schemes (v. 29). This truth could be set forth in a hyperbole: "There is only one in a million (the Hebrew says a "thousand") who acts as he ought" (v. 28). Sin has worked its corrosive effects on the entire human race. Therefore, those who discover wisdom (for that is the subject of this section [vv. 20-29]), are very few indeed.

Why does Solomon appear to lock women out of those few who do find wisdom? "I did not find one woman among all of them," he complained in verse 28. He did not reflect any kind of chauvinism when he wrote in Proverbs 12:4; 14:1; 18:22; and 19:14. In fact, wisdom itself was personified by Solomon as a woman. Had Solomon, for one reason or another, suddenly overlooked the resourcefulness of such women as: "Judge Deborah," the devout Hannah, the prophetic song leader Miriam of the past, or the gifted prophetess Huldah, in his estimate of women?

Solomon does not fit the usual definition of a misogynist— he? A woman hater?! No, that wasn't *his* problem. Some commentators have suggested that this woman, whose heart is here depicted as a snare and a trap (v. 26), is but the personification of that wickedness which is folly itself. She is the "strange woman" of Proverbs 1–9. Perhaps this interpretation is the closest to what Solomon intended, for the topic is wisdom from 7:20 to 8:1. Therefore, never has that seductress been found, the very opposite of the woman wisdom herself, who knows the explanation of these things (8:1). In Ecclesiastes 9:9 Solomon urges a man to "enjoy life with your wife, whom you love", (NIV). In his Proverbs, he is no less complimentary about one's wife (Prov. 12:4; 14:1; 18:22; 19:14; 31:10-31).

Nevertheless, character is not built by multiplied acts of ostentatious worship, nor is it to be presumed to be just naturally a part of all men and women. Unfortunately, just the reverse is true. Foolishness and sin are so much a part of humanity that only by submitting to the Lord in the fear of God will anyone be able to understand both the wisdom of God and the stupidity of wickedness. We are warned, then, that just as we must not "judge a book by its cover," so also we must not presume that the inner character of a person is always what we think it is on the basis of a limited knowledge of the alleged worship of men and women.

## C. 8:2-14 — The Removal of a Large Proportion of the Apparent Inequalities in Divine Providence Comes From *Righteous Government*

Wisdom that comes from the fear of God can solve many present enigmas such as those contemplated in this third section of the book of Ecclesiastes. This divinely sent wisdom is what can dispel the gloom and brighten up what otherwise would be the harsh looks on the faces of those seeking answers.

> ²Obey the king's command, I say, because of the oath of God [you took].
>
> ³Do not be in a hurry to leave him. You may go. Do not stand up for an evil matter, for he does all that he pleases.
>
> ⁴Since the word of a king is supreme, who can say to him, "What are you doing?"
>
> ⁵Whoever obeys his command will come to no harm, and a wise heart will know the [right] time and [proper] justice.
>
> ⁶For to every matter there is a [proper] time and [corresponding] justice, though a man's trouble is heavy upon him.

[7]Since no one knows what will be, who can tell when it will be?

[8]No one has power over the spirit to retain the spirit, and no one has control over the day of death; there is no release in the time of war and wickedness will not deliver those who are owned by it.

[9]All this I saw, as I applied my mind to every deed that is done under the sun. It is a time when man lords it over a man to his hurt.

[10]Then too I have seen the wicked buried (the ones who used to come and go from the holy place) and they worshipped in the city where they did this. This too is perplexing.

[11]When the sentence for an evil deed is not carried out, the hearts of the sons of men are full of evil schemes.

[12]Although a wicked man commits evil deeds a hundred times and prolongs it, I know it will be well with those who fear God and are reverent before him.

[13]But it will not be well for the wicked, and he will not lengthen his days as a shadow, because there is no fear before God.

[14]There is a perplexity that is done upon the earth; there are righteous men to whom it happens according to the deeds of the wicked, and there are wicked men to whom it happens according to the deeds of the righteous. As I have said, this too is perplexing.

A wise man realizes that chief among God's agents of justice, presently available, is the divine institution of human government (8:2-5). The doctrine presented here is exactly the same doctrine as that given by Paul in Romans 13:1-5. Human government is God's ordained means of rectifying many of the current disorders in this life.

Foremost among Solomon's commands in this section is obedience to "the powers that be" (8:2). The reasons for this obedience to a human institution are:

- Subjects are obligated by an oath of allegiance, whether they are foreigners, who are required to give an oath, or native-born citizens, who are also under a covenant to obey (8:2).

- The ruler has authority to enforce what he commands ("He does whatever he pleases" [8:3b-4a]) when subjects get involved in an evil cause.

- There is safety and wisdom in keeping the king's commandment; subjects usually need not "feel any evil thing" (8:5a).

- Wise men are able to discern in their hearts the appropriate time and procedure for doing the king's will (8:5b), for as 3:1 argued, there is an appropriate and divinely appointed time and an adequate procedure for every matter (8:6).

Those arguments are further elaborated in Romans 13:1-7, Titus 3:1, and 1 Peter 2:13-18.

The purpose of government is the righteous administration of justice. When rulers and judges carry out that divine mandate, both they and their people are blessed by God, and a considerable amount of man's present distress is alleviated.

Unfortunately, those in authority are not always faithful to their mandate. In verse 9, it has to be sadly conceded that rulers often inflict injustices on their subjects. This was duly noted by Solomon and provided for in the wise plan of God. Still, in spite of every perversion, God's purpose is accomplished.

The ultimate fulfillment of God's purpose is also the transition point in 8:5b. In language reminiscent of 3:1, we move from human government as God's means of correcting current disorders to God's supreme control over all. The only addition here over the teaching of 3:1 is that besides noting that the excellent plan of God has a set time for everything, Solomon also observes here that there is a judgment set aside for all the wicked (8:6, 13).

Ignorance of the plan and times of God increases man's misery; man is particularly miserable because he cannot avoid death (8:6-8). God has vested the control of all things in His own hands and not in the hands of mortals. And because they are ignorant of God's workings, human beings, not God, are responsible for all the misery endured on earth as they try to do things contrary to God's will.

Even though men and women may be wrongly encouraged in their evil deeds by the abuse of power and position from those in authority (8:9), the wicked receiving honorable burials (8:10) and delays being allowed in the administration of justice (8:11), it will be well nevertheless for those who fear God (8:12-13). "Fear" appears three times in 8:12-13 to denote those who truly and habitually fear and reverence God. There will be a day, as Malachi 3:18 also says, when you will be able to discern the difference between those who feared God and those who refused to fear Him. Then a most exacting justice shall be meted out. The wicked may appear to be getting away with murder ("one hundred times," v. 12), but such sinning with seeming impunity will finally be judged by the Living God.

That the just deserts of the wicked often seem to fall on the righteous God-fearer while the rewards of the righteous appear to drop into the lap of the wicked is understandable only by the wisdom found in the fear of God, the plan of God, and its call to enjoy life as offered by God to any and all who will trust in Him.

The mystery is now solved, so far as its main outlines are concerned. How refreshing, in contrast to the mad search of empty, plastic mortals, who are shaped by their evil desires and the current trends of thought, is the contented capacity of those who fear God to enjoy the gifts given by a loving, all-wise God; to those who have first sought the kingdom of God and His righteousness (8:15; cf. Matt 6:33). God's gift of enjoyment is to be preferred over all accumulations that the wicked possess and for which they are tempted to act so wickedly in obtaining them apart from the plan of God.

In light of the preceding argument, no wonder the Teacher commends joy in his conclusion in 8:15.

> [15]So I commend the enjoyment of life, because there is nothing better for a person under the sun than to eat and drink and be glad. Then joy will accompany them in their toil all the days of the life God has given them under the sun.

It is God alone who keeps him occupied all the days of his life as the great God of the universe answers all the toil and labor mortals do under the sun with His gifts so real and so foundational as eating, drinking, and rejoicing in the work they are given by God. The plan of God has puzzling aspects to it, but it can be applied and explained to a good degree nevertheless, as Solomon has done for us in this central part of his argument.

# 4

# REMOVING DISCOURAGEMENTS TO THE PLAN OF GOD

## *Ecclesiastes 8:16–12:14*

The fourth and final section of Ecclesiastes does not open up new arguments or give particularly new materials; instead, it usually supplements what has already been affirmed. It is true, however, that we are given practical advice and taught how to apply the insights gained from this new perspective on life set forth in the previous three sections. The righteous must be encouraged lest the enigmas or puzzles that still remain in the mystery of God are allowed to dishearten them. In this way the argument of the third section is strengthened and supplemented with practical admonitions.

Once again, this fourth section has three divisions and a conclusion:

A. 8:16–9:9—The Remaining Mystery in This Subject Must Not Diminish Human Joy

B. 9:10–11:6—The Remaining Mystery in This Subject Must Not Prevent Us From Working With All Our Might

C. 11:7–12:7—The Daily Reminder of Our Imminent Death and the Prospect of Facing Our Creator and Judge Should Not Infect All Our God-given Joy and Activity

D. 12:8-14—Conclusion

Rather than beginning with the conclusion as we have done in the previous three sections, we will delay considering the conclusion in this case, since that conclusion also serves as the epilogue for the whole book of Ecclesiastes. Therefore, we will proceed with the same order that is in the text since the general trend of Solomon's argument is clear by now.

## A. 8:16–9:9 — The Remaining Mystery in This Subject Must Not Diminish Human Joy

How vast a scope does the writer's ambitious inquiry into the affairs of men stretch—the total range of man's labor on earth! Yet in spite of all the acknowledged injustice, evil, and crooked deals in the world, man's work is identified with "all the work of God." Now there is a first-class "mystery" in the biblical sense of the word "mystery": something we know somewhat better because of God's disclosure on the subject, but which still contains baffling aspects. Even after we have been treated to an elaborate discussion of the plan of God as it affects the most mundane features of life, and even after we have been warned that the alleged inequalities in the divine plan are often mere hasty inferences made by anxious men, with somewhat shocking, but refreshing, candor, Solomon asserts that there still are some insoluble mysteries in divine providence. Let us examine the text first before we comment on it.

> [16]When I applied my mind to know wisdom and to observe the labor which is done on the earth (though one's eyes see sleep neither day nor night),

> [17]then I saw all that God has done. No one can comprehend what is done under the sun. Despite all his efforts to search it out, he does not find it. Even if a wise man claims he knows, he is not able to comprehend it.

¹So I reflected on all this and I concluded that what the righteous and the wise do are in the hands of God. But no one knows whether love or hate is the entirety of what is before them.

²All share all things alike—the same destiny [comes] to the righteous and the wicked, the good, the clean, the unclean, the one offering sacrifices and the one who does not. As it is with the good man, so it is with the sinner; as it is with the one who takes oaths, so it is with those who are afraid to take an oath.

³This is the evil in all that is done under the sun: the same event comes to all. Moreover, the hearts of men are full of evil, and foolishness is in their hearts while they are alive, but afterward [they join] the dead.

⁴For anyone who is joined to all the living there is hope, for a live dog is better off than a dead lion.

⁵For the living know that they will die, but the dead know nothing; they have no further reward, and even the memory of them is forgotten.

⁶Their love, their hate and even their rivalry have long since vanished; and they will never again have a share in anything that is done under the sun.

⁷Go, eat your bread with joy and drink your wine with a happy heart, for already God has taken pleasure in your works.

⁸Always be clothed in white and do not let your head lack oil.

⁹Enjoy life with your wife, whom you love, all the days of your puzzling life which he has given you under the sun— all your puzzling days. For this is your portion in life, and in your labor, in which you toil under the sun.

No one can know entirely what goes on under the sun (8:17)—only God knows comprehensively and completely. What mortals know is partial and incomplete. Mortals can dig and search for wisdom as much as they wish, but they will discover that they will be as shut out from their desired goal for comprehensive knowledge as the person who went on the same quest for wisdom in Job 28. The author of Job 28 plainly declared: "Man does not know the way to [wisdom]" (Job 28:13), for only "God understands the way" (Job 28:23). In fact, God said to man, "The fear of the Lord, that is wisdom; and to depart from evil is discernment" (Job 28:28). No wonder, then, that even so-called wise men cannot know what goes on under the sun. Human insight, understanding, and reason, like water, cannot rise higher than their source or its own level. Therefore, to the degree that God reveals His plan to believers, to that degree only are they able to *apprehend* that much of the plan of God. Yet there still are mysteries and puzzling aspects that remain. Only God knows entirely; we mortals know only in part.

Should the above concession lead to despair, let it be quickly stated that the righteous and the truly wise, those who fear the Lord, are "in the hands of God" (9:1). The apostle Paul stated the same truth later: "The Lord knows those that are his" (2 Tim. 2:19). Our quest for identity, meaning, and an explanation of the presence of evil, injustice, and inequities in life must end where Solomon's did—in the fact that God sits at the helm, ruling and overruling for good. Consequently, His people, their works, and their very lives are protected and governed by the God who is over all. They are safe in His hands.

## *1. Joy in the Face of Suffering (9:1-6)*

In spite of all that has been said to explain and justify the ways of God to mortals, there still are some mysteries in divine providence. No one can tell just by God's treatment of particular individuals whether they are objects of God's love or hatred (9:1). Qoheleth, the Teacher, warned in 6:1-6 that prosperity is not always or necessarily a good thing, and in 7:1-15 that adversity and affliction are not always or necessarily evil. God's approval or disapproval of us cannot always be read from "all that is before [us]" (9:1); things are not always what they seem to be to us or what our friends construe them to be. After all, Job's three friends took the bare facts of his suffering and incorrectly concluded that he must have sinned grievously; otherwise he would not have been suffering as he was. Nor must we conclude that God hates those to whom he sends adversity and loves those who receive prosperity. If believers are to walk by faith, there will be times when outward appearances and facts will defy explanation for the moment. It is cruel to add to the hurt of oppressed persons by suggesting that they are definitely objects of God's judgment. Such narrow-minded reasoning would suggest that all suffering is the result of personal sin, but that would be unbiblical. Certainly some suffering is (1) *educational* (as Elihu informed Job by divine inspiration in Job 34:32; 35:11; 36:10, 15, 22); some is (2) *doxological,* for the glory of God (as Jesus showed His disciples the proper deduction to be drawn from the man born blind in John 9:1-3); some is (3) *probationary* (as when Habakkuk looked out from his watchtower on a world of tyranny, violence, and sin and found the answer in patient waiting for God's long-suffering retribution to take effect); some is (4) *revelational* (as the prophet Hosea learned in the isolation felt by God as a result of Israel's spiritual adultery when he, Hosea, lost his own wife to physical harlotries); and some suffering is (5) *sacrificial* (as the suffering Servant bore great pain because of the sin of others [Isa. 42; 49–50; 53]). Therefore it is most unfortunate when men hastily make a one-to-one nexus between personal guilt and suffering.

If one argues that this association between suffering and personal guilt is frequently witnessed when the Bible addresses nations and institutions such as bodies of believers, we agree. But local churches do not seem to have any continuing existence in the life to come as local churches; therefore, their judgment must be rendered in God's justice here and now. Individuals, however, will personally stand before God in that day to come.

But to return to the text of Ecclesiastes, the mystery before us in 9:2-6 is the most perplexing of all life's puzzles: how did God ever allow the presence of sin and death in His good world, one which is ruled by His good plan?

Now Solomon does not level a charge against God when he labels what happens to good and evil men alike as an "evil" (9:3). His use of this term "evil," like his evaluation, is strictly from the human point of view and based on appearances. He has, for the moment, purposely left out all considerations of the divine perspective and revelational facts. Thus, so far as men can see, one "event," or "destiny," comes to all.

The word translated "fate," or "fortune" (9:2, 3), in some versions of the Bible, should instead be translated "event" or "happening": "one event comes to all." Solomon refers only to that which "meets" men at the end of their lives, an "event," a "happening," or "outcome" (Hebrew *miqreh*). There is not one hint in this term of anything of the power of fatalism or chance as is found in paganism.

The momentary absence of all distinction between the righteous and the wicked in that all must die is a mystery above all mysteries. Why should profane swearers and irreligious and godless men who abstain from sacrificing and practicing good (9:2) be accorded the same treatment as those who deserve better? It is difficult to understand: the wicked share that "one event" with the good. The wicked, whose hearts are full of evil, and every conceivable madness, while they are alive, join their righteous counterparts as all go to the grave.

Verse 4 makes the point necessary for practical men: where there is life, there is hope. The actual translation of the verse is not as easy as is the sense. The Hebrew and many ancient versions say, "What then is to be chosen? With all the living there is hope." There was, however, a Hebrew tradition of reading (called the *Qere, what is to be "read"*) this text that supposed that two letters ought to be transposed from the *Kethib*, (what is "written") – from the verb "to choose" (*yebuchar*) to make it "to join" (*yechubbar*), – and thus the verse would read, "For whosoever is joined to all the living, he has hope." Both translations are possible, and the sense is not measurably different in either case. (Most commentators and versions have a slight preference for the latter reading.) Solomon's point is plain: While men are still alive there is hope—hope of preparation for meeting God, hope of living significantly, hope of doing something to the glory of God before all men personally face Him as 12:14 warns, when a person will have to give a detailed accounting of his life to determine if it has been lived in a manner well-pleasing to God.

The proverb in verse 4b, a proverb also found in Arabic, reinforces the significance of life. As lowly and despicable a creature as a "dog" is (from the viewpoint of the ancient Near Eastern mentality, dogs were the scavengers of the abandoned garbage of the city), it is still far more preferable to be a live dog than to be a mighty, majestic, exalted—but dead—"lion." Life! That is the precious item!

Gloom seems to settle ever so densely when verses 5-6 are reached. Are these verses a flat denial of any hope for a life beyond the grave? Is it the settled opinion of Qoheleth that when one is dead, he becomes extinct—knowing nothing and finished with everything, including loving, hating, envying, and inheriting?

On the contrary, the reference to all those things is strictly limited to things as they are enjoyed "under the sun" and on this side of immortality. Qoheleth does not deny that men may receive an inheritance in the hereafter, as so many commentators are quick to assert. His point, the same as in John's Gospel, is exceedingly important: "Work while it is still day, for the night comes when no man can work" (John 9:4b). It is the consciousness that men will soon die and no longer be able to relate to the needs and joys of this life that forces the striking contrast of verses 5-6. Knowledge in this life, rewards for this life, and opportunities for service are serious challenges when viewed from the prospect of our soon-to-appear death. If men are going to live as if there is no tomorrow in eternity and let their passions and desires have free reign, they will have played the real fool's role. Thus, although death is still an enigma, men must not pretend to live as if they "only go around once in this world" (to borrow the sorry philosophy of some current Madison Avenue advertising). How sad it would be to have lost all opportunity to share in doing anything significant to the glory of God.

## *2. Joy, the Gift of God and Grace of Life (9:7-9)*

What, then, should be done (9:7-9)? The righteous know: They must rejoice and enjoy life. This is one of the so-called *carpe diem* passages, i.e., "seize the day" (the others are: 2:24-26; 3:12-13, 22; 5:18-20; 8:15), for "this is the day that the Lord has made; [they] will be glad and rejoice in it" (Psalm 118:24). Instead of allowing grief to consume one's life, Solomon urges that whatever remains of the unexplained mystery in our lives must not prevent us from enjoying life. The tendency to brood and to mope has to be resisted in the lives of those who fear God, who take life as a gift from God's hand, and who receive His plan and enablement to enjoy that life.

Accordingly, verse 7 begins with an invitation: "Come on"; "be up and about." To be specific about what it is that one is to do, five pieces of advice are given: (1) eat your food, (2) drink your wine, (3) get out your white set of clothes, (4) shampoo your head with the most luxurious of oils, and (5) enjoy the domestic comfort and love of your wife (9:7-9). The reason for such action is stated immediately: "For God has already accepted your works" (9:7, NKJV). Righteous men need not worry whether God is indifferent to them and their lives: He is not; they are the special objects of His gifts and His acceptance.

The text is clear about the word "already," (*kebar*), which the NIV tried to soften with "for it is *now* that God favors what you do," using the word "now" for "already" and using the imperfect or uncompleted form of the verb rather than the past or completed form of the verb *ratsah*, "to approve." But if pre-approval of human acts equals empowerment, then as Ecclesiastes 5:16 and 6:2 had previously noted, often God keeps the gift of the possessions separate from the gift of enjoyment of those things so that mortals might be forced to reckon with Him as the giver and maintainer of the gifts. Ecclesiastes 5:16 and 6:2 used the word *hishlit*, "to empower." W. Sibley Towner makes the fine point that "Long ago God had declared it to be morally correct that human beings should enjoy bread, wine and life itself... God created human life good from the beginning and wills that human beings take legitimate pleasure in being alive."[1]

Wine and bread, the staff of life, are frequently representative in Scripture of that which God gives to comfort and cheer us (Gen. 14:18; 1 Sam. 16:20; 25:18; Neh. 5:15; Eccles. 10:19; Lam. 2:12). Likewise, white garments and ointments were symbols of joy and purity, as John illustrated in his word to the Church of Sardis in Revelation 3:4-5:

> You have a few persons, even in Sardis, who have not defiled their garments; they shall walk with me in white: for they are worthy. He that overcomes, the same shall be clothed in white clothing (cf. Rev. 19:8).

Because ordinary people could not maintain and perpetually clean their cool and pleasant white garments as could people of wealth and rank, they reserved such clothes for especially important or festive occasions. Accordingly, white garments became emblems of joy and festivity. The same was true of perfuming, or anointing, oneself with oils.

Neither is the joy of marriage to be left out of life. Celibacy, or abstinence, is not a holier state than matrimony, for the point Qoheleth is making is the same as that of the

---

1    W. Sibley Towner, "The Book of Ecclesiastes," in *The New Interpreter's Bible* (Nashville: TN: Abingdon Press, 1997), 12 vols., 5:340.

writer of the book of Hebrews: marriage is honorable and the marriage bed is undefiled (Heb. 13:4). So, to the festive delights of verses 7-8, Solomon adds the gratifications, comforts, and delights of enjoying life with your wife whom you love (9:9). Literally, the Hebrew text reads: *"See* life with the wife you love" (emphasis added). This expression "to see" was used in a more comprehensive manner than we use it today in the West. Ginsburg said that the verb "to see" was used of those who were in the midst of experiencing any of the full range of human emotions and passions (e.g., see Eccles. 2:1).[2] Thus Solomon's advice is to go ahead, get married, and enjoy the delights of married love and companionship instead of worrying about the remaining mystery in the plan of God. Do not even try to fully comprehend why you enjoy the gifts mentioned in verses 7-9. Receive them for what they are, gifts, and receive God's ability to partake of them with pleasure. Would not Peter add later that beautiful instruction to husbands: "Live considerately with your wives...since you are joint heirs of the grace of life" (1 Pet. 3:7)?

The tone of this injunction sets the context for understanding Solomon's earlier word on women in 7:26-28. He was definitely not a misogynist. He was fully aware of what a beautiful gift a true, faithful wife is. Men should abstain from marriage only if they are given the gift of celibacy (1 Cor. 7:7) or if the times are so perilous that marriage would be an added pressure and not a joy (Jer. 16:1-4; 1 Cor. 7:26, 29).

---

2    Christian D. Ginsburg, *Coheleth, Commonly Called the Book of Ecclesiastes* [1861; reprinted in *The Song of Songs and Coheleth (Commonly Called the Book of Ecclesiastes)*, The Library of Biblical Studies, edited by Harry M. Orlinsky (New York: Ktav, 1970), p. 276.

Be joyful, then, and receive God's gifts and His ability to enjoy them. Why should anyone who truly fears God have the joy of life stolen out from under them because of the unresolved perplexities still remaining in the partially[3] disclosed plan of God? Rejoice and be exceedingly glad, for these are the gifts that the Lord has made; we should rejoice and be glad in them (to paraphrase the words of Psalm 118:24). To be sure, the "joy of the Lord is [our] strength" (Neh. 8:10), and in that stronghold and tower the righteous take refuge during life's journey.

Qoheleth urges acceptance of the grace and joy of life, not pessimism, nihilism, and blind determinism. Believers are to be rebuked for rejecting God's worldly gifts and refusing to use them in a proper way. Out of a distorted view of worldliness, wherein every pleasure ordained by God for man's enjoyment is either denied or begrudgingly used, many have developed a super-pious, unhappy, and even miserable existence. This text proclaims liberation to them. Brother and sister: rejoice in God's good gifts, and ask for His ability rightfully to use them. Accordingly, neither our joy nor our involvement in work is to be short-circuited because of all inability to explain everything in life or the world.

## B. 9:10–11:6 — The Remaining Mystery in This Subject Must Not Prevent Us From Working with All Our Might

[10]Whatever your hand finds to do, do it with all your might, for there is no working, planning, knowledge, or wisdom where you are going in the grave.

---

3   Christian D. Ginsburg, *Coheleth, Commonly Called the Book of Ecclesiastes* p. 276.

[11]I turned and I saw under the sun that the race is not to the speedy or the battle to the strong, nor does food come to the wise, or riches to the brilliant, or favor to the learned; for time and events happen to them all.

[12]A human being does not know his time: as fish are caught in a cruel net, or birds are taken in a snare, so human beings are entrapped by evil times, that fall unexpectedly upon them.

[13]I also experienced this [piece of] wisdom under the sun that greatly impressed me.

[14][There once was] a small city with a few peope in it. And a great king came against it, surrounded it and built huge siege-works against it.

[15]Now there lived in that city a poor, but wise man, and he saved that city by his wisdom. But no one remembered that poor man.

[16]So I concluded, wisdom is better than strength, but the poor man's wisdom is despised, and his words are not heard.

[17]The calm words of the wise are more to be heeded than the shouts of a ruler of fools.

[18]Wisdom is better than the weapons of war, but one sinner destroys much good.

[1]As dead flies make a perfumer's oil turn rancid and ferment, so a little folly outweighs wisdom and honor.

[2]The heart of the wise inclines to the right, but the heart of the fool to the left.

[3]Even as the fool walks along the road, he lacks sense and shows to everyone how stupid he is.

[4]If the anger of the ruler rises against you, do not leave your post; calmness can lay to rest great offenses.

⁵There is an evil I have seen under the sun, an error that proceeds from the ruler:

⁶Fools are put in many high positions while the rich sit in a low place.

⁷I have seen slaves on horseback while princes go like servants on foot.

⁸Whoever digs a pit may fall into it; whoever breaks through a stone wall may be bitten by a snake.

⁹Whoever quarries stones may be hurt by them; whoever splits logs may be endangered by them.

¹⁰If the ax is dull and its edge unsharpened, more strength is needed. Skill has the advantage of granting success.

¹¹If the snake bites before being enchanted, there is no profit to the master of the tongue.

¹²Words from a wise man's mouth are gracious, but the lips of a fool confound him.

¹³At the beginning the words of his mouth are folly, but at the end his words are wicked foolishness—

¹⁴and the fool multiplies words. No one knows what is to be and who can tell him what will happen after him?

¹⁵The toil of a fool wearies him; he does not know how to get to the city.

¹⁶Woe to you, O land, when your king is a child and whose princes feast in the morning.

¹⁷Blessed are you, O land, when your king is the son of nobles and your princes eat at an appropriate time—for strength and not for drunkenness.

¹⁸Through laziness the rafters sag, and through idleness of [his] hands the house leaks.

[19]A feast is made for laughter, and wine makes life joyful, but money is the answer to everything.

[20]Do not curse the king even in your thoughts, and do not curse the rich in your bedroom; for a bird of the air may carry [your] voice and [a bird] on wings will report what you say.

[1]Cast your bread on the waters, for after many days you may find it.

[2]Give a portion to seven, even to eight, for you do not know what evil may come upon the land.

[3]If the clouds are full of rain, they empty out upon the land; and if a tree falls to the south or to the north, in the place where it falls, there it will be.

[4]Whoever watches the wind will not plant; whoever looks at the clouds will not harvest.

[5]As you do not know the way of the Spirit, how bones grow in the womb, so you cannot understand the work of God who makes everything.

[6]In the morning sow your seed and at evening do not let your hands be idle, for you do not know which will succeed, whether this or that, or whether both will do equally well.

## 1. Work While It Is Yet Day (9:10-12)

The time to labor for God is while we are still on this side of the grave, for when death comes, the day of opportunity will have passed. The phrasing of verse 10 is reminiscent of Colossians 3:23: "Whatever your task, do it heartily, as unto the Lord and not to men." Men must not opt out of total, earnest, and dedicated involvement in the privilege of work. They may think that the presence of evil and their impending death are massive obstacles to believing that God has a good plan for all of life, and therefore they may refuse to do anything pending further disclosures on the subject. But such inactivity is wrong. Counsels the Teacher, "Get involved and work vigorously" to the glory of God while you still have life in your bones.

Once again, Solomon warns, "There is no work, no planning, no knowledge, and no wisdom in the grave [*Sheol*] where you are going" (9:10). But as in 9:5-6, so here: this affirmation is no denial of a future state, or of personal, conscious presence with God immediately after death of the body. The point is that in relation *to this world* (9:6), those possibilities have ceased. To make the words of 9:10 into an absolute denial of immortality would be as unfair as doing the same to Jesus' words in John 9:4: "The night comes when no man can work."

The Hebrew word *Sheol* occurs about sixty-five times in the Old Testament and is already correctly translated as "grave" in approximately half of those instances in most of our English translations. In my judgment, all sixty-five could be equally well rendered "grave." This does not deny the existence of the doctrine of a separate place for the departed, unbelieving dead, namely, "hell"; it only raises the question whether this particular word should be translated that way in all or any of its contexts. Certainly in this verse the rendering "grave" fills the bill well.

Therefore, while the resources of life are still at hand— ability to *do* work, faculties to *devise,* or brainstorm, new ideas, and ability to use the almost daily accumulation of knowledge and *wisely* apply it to the situations of life (9:10)—put your whole self and strength into each task.

To further stimulate men to action, Solomon makes three supporting arguments that may be stated in the following proverbs (9:11-12):

- It is not in the man himself that walks to direct his steps (Jer. 10:23).

- The Lord may save by many or by few (1 Sam. 14:6).

- Time and events [destiny] come to all (Eccles. 9:11).

Advantages and resources often mean very little if God is not in those talents. In quick order Solomon ticks off five assets enjoyed by men who would appear to be the most likely to succeed: the "swift," the "strong," the "wise," the "discerning," and the "learned." To use Biblical examples, who was swifter than, Asahel, who fell needlessly, smitten by the butt end of Abner's spear (2 Sam. 2:22-23)? Who was stronger than Samson, but who was weaker before women (Judg. 16:19)? Who was wiser than Solomon, but who was more indulgent in sin? (1 Kings 11:1-25)? Who was more discerning than Ahithophel, but who was so easily supplanted by Hushai and his foolish counsel (2 Sam. 16:23; 17:5-14)? Who was more learned in all the ways of the Egyptians than Moses, yet who also pre-empted every agency of justice in rushing into murder (Exod. 2:11-15; Acts 7:22)?

In the divine plan, the race belongs to the one who runs in the strength of God. Strength, wisdom, speed, discernment, and learning are only valuable insofar as they are ordered by God. "Time and events happen to them all" (9:11), observed Qoheleth. The second subject of the sentence, "events," is not to be rendered "chance." The word (Hebrew *pega'*) simply means an "occurrence" and comes from the verb "to meet" (cf. 1 Kings 5:4). It is true, however, that the "occurrence," or "event," is usually an *evil* occurrence. Because the verb shared by this compound subject is singular (*yiqreh,* "to come, happen"), the idea is a compact one. The "time" is a time of judgment to be directed by God, in which He may allow the events and situations of life to overwhelm and overthrow those whose endowment of abilities seems to deny the possibility of their ever failing. It is a vain thing to trust in any human qualities rather than in the living God. The same truth is taught in Proverbs 21:30, "There is no wisdom, no discernment, and no counsel that can prevail against the Lord"; and in 1 Samuel 17:47, "The Lord does not deliver with the sword or the spear, for the battle belongs to the Lord" (see also 2 Chron. 20:15).

Human ability cannot guarantee success. In fact, more frequently than not, those who trust the most in their own abilities are the very persons who are caught unsuspectingly and suddenly by their own devices. Those who appear to be doing so well in this life end up being the greatest losers around. "If we could see beyond today as God can see," sang the songwriter. But we would conclude his song somewhat differently to fit the truth here: "Then we would not begin to doubt and often complain." When men do not pay attention to the fact that their "time" of judgment is ever near, they are trapped, just as fish and birds are caught in nets (v. 12). Believers must not judge these books by the covers; things are not what they appear to be. God is in charge. Men will be judged. Men must diligently work with all their might to the glory of God in every aspect of life, for the night is coming when the opportunity will be lost and all of life will be reviewed by the God who knows absolutely what is right and what is wrong.

## 2. God-Given Wisdom is of the Utmost Importance in Our Work (9:13-18)

As an illustration of the great advantage to be found in the employment of wise action, a parable is cited in 9:13-16. The situation is one of remarkable contrast: a small city with few persons in it was besieged by a great king with the latest in armaments and military might. But the apparently unstoppable king was outmaneuvered. There was in that same besieged city a poor, but wise, man who delivered the small city from the great king. The shame of the matter was that no one remembered who the wise man was; neither was he ever properly honored or rewarded. Thus, although that poor, wise man failed to profit personally from his labors, his wisdom was not profitless for others or for this world.

The conclusions to be drawn from this parable are found in 9:16-18. (1) Wisdom, that gift that comes from the fear of God (Prov. 1:7, 29; 2:5; 8:13; 15:33), is a greater asset than strength, even though it is often despised and left unheeded by the masses (9:16a). Such a triumph of wisdom over brute force as in the parable of 9:13-16 was no doubt fresh in Solomon's mind. For when David's general, Joab, besieged the small city of Abel in Israel, where the insurrectionist Sheba had taken hasty refuge, a wise woman called to Joab from the city wall and delivered the city in her wisdom (2 Sam. 20:16-22).

The other side of the coin is that (2) wisdom is not always heeded (9:16b). Only in emergencies can the quiet words of wisdom be heard. Therefore, (3) men must have a certain mental disposition and spirit of receptivity if wisdom is to be heard (9:17). The clamor of demagogues and self-styled bosses is a striking contrast to words of quiet instruction delivered by wise men of God. (4) "Wisdom is power," to restate an old proverb, but one sinner (or ruler) who in his folly and self-willed obstinacy refuses to accept "wisdom" thereby destroys much good and many a kingdom, too (9:18).

## 3. Results of Foolish and Wise Works Are Contrasted (10:1-20)

To reinforce his admonition about the value of wisdom, Solomon in chapter 10 exhibits the same thought in a series of loosely connected maxims in the style found in the book of Proverbs 10–29. Just as we argued that 3:2-8 does not refer to various stages in a Christian's growth process, or even to seven periods or ages in the church, so chapter 10 is not a chapter of connected teachings on rulers (vv. 4-7, 16-17, 20), or the evils of ill-conceived attempts to overthrow bad governments (vv. 8-10, 18-19).

Therefore, what 10:1 does is to illustrate the last statement in 9:18 from an everyday incident. Just as one "dead fly" (or, more accurately, "flies that bring death," i.e., by their excrement) affects the entire batch of costly ointment, so a little folly can display itself as mightier and more glorious than the genuine wisdom of a poor, wise man who could deliver his small city from the hands of a great king. There is a related Arabic proverb: "A fly is nothing, yet it produces loathsomeness." So a little bit of foolishness, although as insignificant as a fly (we would say a flea), is nonetheless able to muster great power in the eyes of men. Solomon does not refer to that trace of folly in a wise man or the lapses of the otherwise good man; he instead refers to the tendency for folly to predominate over "honorable wisdom" (note in the Hebrew for 10:1b the word *min,* meaning "than," or "a comparison").

But appearances must not deceive believers, for the "heart" (i.e., the mind, or inner nature) of a wise man is ever ready to protect him from numerous dangers (10:2)— on his right hand. The right hand is not a reference to good luck and the left to ill fortune, for the Bible has no belief in such a goddess of fortune. As Ginsburg noted, to be on one's right was to defend or be ready to assist one,[4] as in Psalm 16:8 and 121:5. To keep men from concluding that wisdom was *absolutely* useless, Solomon again qualified that implication by showing wisdom's relative advantages and merits. The fool, meanwhile, "misses his mind," or is absent from it. His heart and mind are useless to him in emergencies.

The fool exposes himself as soon as he sets foot outside his door (10:3). Whether "on the way" is meant literally or figuratively (for his lifestyle and dealings with men) makes little difference. In all of life, he openly proclaims that he is a fool to all who meet him. Wisdom is much more to be preferred than all of this in verses 1-3.

But another issue arises in 10:4-7; namely, the wisdom of patiently submitting to the anger of tyrannical rulers because, as 8:16-17 stated at the beginning of this section, men are not always able to tell just why certain things are done. The wisdom embodied in verse 4 was later expressed, as Genung observed,[5] in the beatitude, "Blessed are the meek" (Matt. 5:5). Solomon had taught the same truth in Proverbs 16:14, and the subject of his remarks, no

---

4   Ginsburg, *Coheleth*, p. 425.

5   John F. Genung, *Words of Koheleth* (New York: Houghton, Mifflin and Co., 1904), p. 331.

doubt, was not his own royal practices, but the practices of those who ruled in the countries around Israel.

In this connection of pacifying anger aroused by great errors, "There is an evil," says Qoheleth in one of his favorite introductory phrases (10:5; cf. 5:13; 6:9). Yet in line with the wise and meek attitude he has just counseled in the preceding verse (v. 4), he continues, "Such an error" gives evidence that not everything rulers do is always perfect and fair. This blot on the record of human governments is another one of those enigmas in the divine plan: Why does God allow such foolishness to continue?

The blunder and error of human governments can often be seen in this tragedy: rulers put their foolish favorites into office over those who are more qualified (10:5-6). Such strangers to the fear of God are called fools. Meanwhile, those who by birth and training are more qualified for such government posts are passed by. These errors are the natural fruit of partiality, tyranny, and despotism. If the ruler had used wisdom, he would have chosen the "nobles" (literally "the rich"), whose ability to accumulate and handle wealth might have indicated the gifts of prudence and wisdom.

The arbitrariness of despotism is indicated by the frequent reversal of positions among the citizenry. In a culture in which only dignitaries were allowed the privilege of riding, there was great social upheaval, as suggested by the complete reversal of normal roles—servants were riding horses while princes walked like menials at their side (10:7). Many have longed to know why such things are allowed by God to happen. If only—. But that is one part of God's plan that He has not been pleased to reveal to us in detail. The reality of such arbitrariness is freely granted by the text, but the text also warns us against permitting it to become a roadblock to joyful and active involvement in life.

No less disturbing are the series of difficulties posed in 10:8-11. The connection of thought between these verses and what preceded can be explained in any number of ways: (1) as Solomon's warnings against participating in the overthrow of despotic governments; (2) as a discussion of the difficulty of governing the masses; (3) as a reminder that life is determined by what some call fate and not the wisdom of men; and (4) as a description of the unenviable end of those young upstarts who try to buck the system. Actually, however, the theme is still the contrasting results of the application of wisdom or folly to life's difficult situations. The key word in the preceding set of proverbs was patience. Wise, wholehearted activity will be tempered by meekness, or "patience" (Hebrew *marpe*). But in verses 8-11, the keyword is "success" (Hebrew *haksher*), which wise action brings (v. 10b).

The warning of the five sentences preceding the concluding observation of 10:10b is that every course of action in life has its risk. If one is to succeed and emerge with "benefit," or "profit" (cf. the theme question of 1:3: "What's the *benefit* of all man's labor?"), he must act, but act wisely. That is the "margin" that counts. There is the "surplus" (*yitron*). The balance of power, observes Genung, is wisdom.[6] Wise men, unlike fools, take into their calculations the possible danger, and then they guard against it. The situations and their dangers are ordinary enough:

---

6    Genung, *Words of Koheleth*, p. 333.

| Situations | Dangers |
|---|---|
| 1. Digging pits | 1. Falling into the pits |
| 2. Breaking down walls | 2. Being bitten by a serpent |
| 3. Quarrying stones | 3. Being hurt by the stones |
| 4. Splitting logs | 4. Endangering oneself |
| 5. Chopping wood | 5. Overexertion because of a dull ax |

Wisdom is the difference between success and failure. It allows for something "left over," a "surplusage" and an "advantage" that contributes to the success of the task and the character of the worker. And wisdom must not be an afterthought added to one's work as perfume is added to complete the dressed-up person. Ecclesiastes 10:11 bemoans the uselessness of help that comes too late, like a charmer (or, as we would say, the snake handler) who comes after the viper has already bitten someone. To use another proverb, why lock the barn door after the cow has gotten out? The proper and wise use of the charmer's tongue could have prevented the disaster and been of "benefit" (*yitron*) to the afflicted.

Appropriately enough, there now follows a series of proverbs on using the tongue wisely while fools prattle away emptily (10:12-15). Wisdom is still the only proper guide to joyful involvement in life, despite life's pitfalls and inexplicable twists. Wisdom will temper, guard, and guide our actions—that is, true wisdom found in the fear of God. And the instrument of this wisdom will be the tongue, or words, of a wise man. His words are gracious in content, winsome in spirit, affectionate in appeal, and compliant and affable in tone.

On the other hand, the words of a fool work his own defeat and destruction—they "swallow him up" (10:12b, NKJV). He is his own worst enemy. His words may be portrayed in a sort of gradation, where at first he is guilty of no more than mere silliness or nonsense;[7] but as he goes on from one folly to the next, he ends up in all sorts of extremism. There is nothing by which he can measure or guide his speech—it becomes sheer madness (10:13). He simply talks too much (10:14a), a constant stream of foolishness.

The pity is that the fool has no idea what he is talking about. He has no idea what the future holds. His unbelief and failure to consider that there is a future judgment, wherein the totality of life will be reviewed, puts him at such a huge disadvantage compared to the devout, wise man that he is to be pitied.

The rhetorical question about the fool's lack of knowledge of the future, or his deficiency in the area of some teacher who should tell him about the future (10:14b), is a valid reminder of a repeated Solomonic theme. The same question had been asked in 3:22, 6:12, 8:7, and in part in 9:12, to prepare the true seeker after God for the grand conclusion of 12:14: God—He alone—will bring every deed into judgment, whether good or evil. Foolish babblers are a dime a dozen, but revelation that is "in the know" is difficult to come by unless a wise man (12:9-11) teaches words of truth about man's future.

A fool will exert himself until he is blue in the face (and in vocabulary), but he will have little more effect than to tire

---

7    Genung, *Words of Koheleth*, p. 334.

men (10:15a). People will get sick of a self-styled religious demagogue's proclaiming God's death and the futility of any hope beyond the grave. The fool's lack of knowledge and discretion on such topics will be plain from his lack of good horse sense in any other area. If he doesn't know how to get from his place to town (10:15b), how can he be trusted when he pontificates on such topics as the hereafter? He is all talk. Genung described the fool's prattle in the words of Shakespeare's Macbeth, as "a tale / Told by an idiot, full of sound and fury, / Signifying nothing.[8]

Once more Qoheleth will enlist the services of wisdom in a fresh effort to aid men in the happy improvement of their lives (10:16-20). With adroitness and the utmost care, Solomon warns that his previous discussion about the wisdom of obeying kings should not be taken as a blank check of approval for everything princes and rulers do. In verse 16, instead of directly attacking the ruler and princes, he denounces the "land" whose king is so foolish as to be childish and whose princes are so bold as to begin their drinking parties in the morning. Nevertheless, his meaning is clear: "Woe" to *them*.

But how fortunate is that land in which the king and his staff rule with wisdom (10:17)! Continuing the sad state of affairs in verse 16, verse 18 decries those rulers who indulge in luxury and intemperance, allowing the country to deteriorate and permitting abuses to flourish. Such a dilapidated and reckless maintenance of justice must be compared to the leaking of a house's roof, causing the roof to rot and, ultimately, collapse. This evil can be laid at the feet of one form of foolishness—downright laziness.

---

8    Genung, *Words of Koheleth*, p. 336.

The land's misfortune through such foolishness is further compounded in 10:19 by the people's idleness and indulgence in laughter, feasts, and drinking, and money is their solution to everything: "Money answers every demand and every wish."

But as if to quickly caution the wise person not to be tempted to unwisely make a frontal attack on government just because some or most of the leaders lack credibility, Solomon adds verse 20. Be careful of disloyal speech that comes from disloyal thoughts. Influential members of the body politic may learn of your thoughts when some unseen event exposes you. The proverbial reference to the bird in verse 20 is like our proverb, "The walls have ears," or "Some little bird told me." Thus Solomon advises discretion, caution, and control.

## 4. Active Involvement Is Proper, Even When Success Is Not Guaranteed in Every Case (11:1-6)

Since we cannot comprehend the totality of God's providential acts, the only proper course of action is to be diligent and wholeheartedly involved; some of this activity will succeed even if all of it does not.

Serving as illustrations of this general advice, Solomon lists a half-dozen everyday incidents to describe what he means. In 11:1 he advises that men "cast their bread on the waters," even when there is no assurance that they will benefit from that action. Indeed, they may "find it after many days," but nothing is guaranteed.

Delitzsch quotes a similar Aramaic proverb of Ben Sira: "Scatter thy bread on the water and on the dry land; in the end of the days thou findest it again." And there is a similar Arabic proverb: "Do good, cast thy bread into the water, thou shalt be repaid some day."[9]

As Ginsburg observed, Solomon, having just given us proverbs for dealing wisely with those *above us,* now gives us a proverb for dealing with those *below us.*[10] Thus, he is encouraging hospitality and patient trust in the ultimate rewards of God according to His master plan. The "bread on the water" may not be a literal reference to throwing thin cakes of bread into the water like chips of wood in the hope that those cakes will one day turn up in some distant place where we will be—and there be in need of bread cakes! The figure may come instead from the realm of foreign commerce, wherein ships finally return with a gain, after an indefinite period of time. Likewise, men and women must judiciously and courageously venture forth in benevolent charity without selfish motives, for such help must be given with the confidence that there is a dependable order and plan in the world and a "God who does all."

As if to make plain his meaning in verse 1, Qoheleth repeats his thought and develops it in verse 2. What had been said in the figure of "cast thy bread on the waters" is now said plainly and literally: "Give a portion to seven, even to eight." Of course, the numbers here are not to limit such generosity to only eight individuals, nor are they an indication of uncertainty—seven or eight. Rather, this is the scriptural pattern of "x + 1," as, for example, in Amos 1 and 2: "For three transgressions, yea four." "Be

---

9    Franz Delitzsch, *Commentary on the Song of Songs and Ecclesiastes*, trans. M. G. Easton (1877; reprinted in *Commentary on the Old Testament*, C. F. Keil and Franz Delitzsch, Grand Rapids: Eerdmans, 1950), p. 391.

10   Ginsburg, p. 447.

liberal and generous to as *many* as you can and *then some"* is the way we would say it. So, make as many friends as you can, for you never know when you yourself may need assistance. Instead of becoming miserly just because you fear that the future may hold some evil reversal of your fortunes, leaving you in poverty and want, you should all the more distribute to as many as possible so that you can have the blessing of receiving in the event of such reverses. In fact, says Proverbs 19:17, "The one who had pity on the poor lends to the Lord; and that which he gives, will be paid back again." (See also Luke 16:9.)

A third illustration is found in 11:3, which also urges us to continued activity even though we are ignorant of the circumstances connected with our exertions. Full clouds will empty themselves on the earth even though some of the water seems to be wasted, falling on lakes, oceans, and uninhabited deserts. But some of the rain will be directly beneficial. Likewise, trees blown over in storms will fall on one man's property or another's. But someone will get the use of the firewood, so rejoice.

Similarly, man cannot tell what will come from any event in life. Yet the believer knows that whether he receives the evil of a flood, hurricane, tornado, or famine, or the blessing of a rich harvest, the seasonal showers, or an unexpected gift or inheritance; they all come from the hand of a God who does or permits them all. So what if we cannot prognosticate the outcome of all our joyful involvement in life's tasks? Is not this detail also covered in the plan of God? Men who insist on certainties or even just the most favorable conditions prior to acting in life never will do anything (11:4). The farmer who hesitates too much over threatening wind and clouds will never get down to sowing and reaping. Again, the duty is ours; the results are God's. Of course, this proverb must not be directed against careful observation of surrounding conditions. Rather, it is aimed at the fruitless and impossible demand for absolute certainty in conditions before we act.

In like manner, 11:5 continues, saying that no one knows the way of the wind or the way bones are formed in a mother's womb; so it may be stated that even though the plan of God is known in general, "The work of God who accomplishes all" lies beyond our knowledge. No one can penetrate the wholeness or the specific details of His work. How God works out His purposes in detail may escape us, but our ignorance does not stop the result, nor should it prevent our wholehearted involvement in life to the glory of God.

Twice in verses 5 and 6 the phrase occurs, "You do not know." But the key to this section is the phrase in verse 6, "Withhold not your hand", (ESV). Let the result—be it success or failure—rest in the hand of God. But do not just sit there, waiting for secure guarantees for life. Do something now, right where you are.

Thus Solomon has repeatedly coaxed, urged, argued, pressed, and begged us as wise men and women to get off the dead center of attempting to outguess God and His works. We must earnestly and diligently get into life's work. It is enough to know, as far as the progress and results of our work are concerned, that God is also at work. It is enough to know that He has given us the knowledge of the broad spectrum of His plan. Therefore, we will not deliberately withhold our energies or refrain from working. That small amount of admitted mystery in the divine plan will not hinder us from becoming active in life to the glory of God.

## C. 11:7–12:8 — The Daily Reminder of Our Imminent Death and the Prospect of Facing Our Creator and Judge Should Not Infect All Our God-given Joy and Activity

### *1. Enjoy the Present and Look Forward to the Future (11:7-10)*

[7]Light is sweet and it is good for the eyes to see the sun.

[8]However many years a person may live, let him enjoy them all; but let him remember the days of darkness, for they will be many. All that is coming is transitory.

[9]Rejoice young man in your youth and let your heart do you good in the days of your childhood; walk in the ways of your heart and the sight of your eyes, but know that for all these God will bring you into judgment.

[10]Therefore, banish anxiety from your heart and put away evil from your flesh, for childhood and vigor are transitory.

Rejoice, shouts our learned guide, in all of life (11:7-9). Yet just as quickly he warns that the quality of life must be such that it will pass muster before the final Judge of all persons and deeds. Our present life was meant to be joyous, as pleasant to the eyes as the rising sun in the morning light (11:7), but with the consciousness that we must render an account unto God for all of life. And if we should live many years, verse 8 counsels that we should enjoy them all. Yet our eyes must be directed to those inevitable days of disease and death when we must go to the grave and then to meet our Maker and Fruit Inspector-Judge. Thus our writer begins his finale as he winds up his massive argument on God and culture, man and meaning.

Verse 9 has been taken in two different ways. One view takes the phrase "Walk in the ways of your heart" as a direct contradiction of Numbers 15:39b: "You shall ... not follow after your own heart and your own eyes" (ESV, cf. Deut. 29:19; Job 31:7). Verse 9, however, is no contradiction to Numbers 15:39b or invitation to live sinfully in sensual pleasure.

The second view of 11:9 is to be preferred. It says the verse is an invitation to youth to get all the cheer and joy they can out of innocent happiness. Yes, enjoy whatever you see or desire, but *mark it down well* and in the midst of your enjoyment remember that God will review even the quality of your pleasures and the manner in which you enjoy yourself. Verse 9 is no *carte blanche* or open season in which *anything goes*. Therefore, do not abuse this blessing with evil comforts and pleasures that offer no real joy. Real but innocent and pure pleasures are recommended. Life must be lived with eternity's values in view. Your one life will soon be past, and only what is done for Christ and with eyes fixed on Christ will last. So have fun! Rejoice and delight yourself in the thrill of living. Yet put a prudent tone into your step by recalling that today will reappear in the tomorrow when we face the One who fully knows right from wrong.

Having shown in 11:7-9 that true happiness consists of simultaneously enjoying the present and looking forward to the future, Qoheleth now tells us how to regulate our lives accordingly. To enjoy true happiness we must remove all anxiety, sorrow, and sadness from our minds, for youth and life itself are so "transient," or "fleeting" (*hebel*, 11:10). End all sadness, fretting, and morose gloom. Men must be free from those injuries to the inner man that so quickly cripple the joy of life.

## *2. Remember to Live for Your Creator Before Death Overtakes You (12:1-7)*

[1]Remember your Creator in the days of your youth, before the days of trouble come and the years approach when you say, "I have no pleasure in them."

[2]Before the sun and the light and the moon and the stars grow dark and the clouds return after the rain,

[3]In the day when the keepers of the house tremble, and the heroic men are bent, when the grinders cease because they are few, and those looking through the windows grow dim;

[4]when the doors on the street are closed and the sound of the grinding mill fades; when one rises up at the sound of a bird, and all the daughters of song are brought low;

[5]when men are afraid of heights and of terrors on the road; when the almond tree blossoms, and the grasshopper drags along, and the caper-berry is useless, for the person goes to his eternal home and mourners go about the streets;

[6]before the silver cord is severed, or the golden bowl is broken; before the pitcher is shattered at the spring, or the wheel is shattered at the well;

[7]and the dust returns to the earth as it was, and the spirit returns to God who gave it.

As Solomon concludes his treatise on how life is to be enjoyed as it was planned by God, he begs men and women to avoid future sorrow and evil by determining to "remember" their Creator in their youth (12:1). When he uses the word "remember," he is not asking for mere mental cognizance, for the biblical term "to remember" means much more than a simple or mere act of mental recall. Besides reflecting on and pondering the work of God in creating each individual and his world, there is the strong implication of action. For example, when God "remembered" Hannah (1 Sam. 1:19), He did more than say, "Oh yes, Hannah; I almost forgot you." When he remembered her, He *acted* decisively on her behalf, and she who was barren conceived the child Samuel. So it is in our passage. To remember our Creator calls for decisive *action* based on the mental recollection of and reflection on all that God is doing and has done for us. That action must go way beyond the cognitive act of calling something to mind: it must result in an action appropriate to that recollection.

With one of the most beautiful of all allegories in Scripture, using the picture of an old, decaying house, Qoheleth sets forth strong reasons for men and women to begin acting decisively in strenuous activity to the glory of their Creator *before* the evil days draw near. Indeed, already in 12:1 he has given three reasons why men must now work: (1) God is Creator of all; (2) He is their Creator; and (3) there are evil days coming when the body's strength and mental capacities will begin to fail, and thus the output and potential for service to the living God will diminish significantly.

The next verses (12:2-6) detail this progressive dissipation in a most eloquent series of poetic pictures. Countless analogies have been suggested, but two principal ones usually emerge. One view sees verses 2-6 as a description of an approaching Palestinian storm that puts a stop to all business and causes all (masters, servants, men, women, and children alike) to quake. The second and more probable view, if a single interpretation of the analogy is to be used, is that the imagery of a decaying and unprotected house pictures the progressive decay that is coming on the bodily members.

The cloudy day following the showers in 12:2 is, according to the prevalent symbolism of the Old Testament, a day, or time, of pending misfortune (cf. Joel 2:2; Zeph. 1:15). And the darkening of the sun, moon, and stars of verse 2, although more difficult to render than almost anything else in this allegory, possibly stands for those first signs of failure in a man's memory, understanding, will, affections, and imaginations. Delitzsch has a long proof in which he tries to equate "the sun" with the soul and "the moon" with the spirit, or principle of life in the body; and he says that "the stars" may refer to the five planets, that is, the five senses.[11] The attempt is ingenious enough, but it seems to be a bit overdone.

The general idea of what is happening in this verse can still be proclaimed, however: one *mental* and internal infirmity after another begins at the sunset of life (to use another metaphor), hampering our effectiveness in serving our Creator. Consequently, we would be well-advised to get moving ("remembering") while those evil days have not yet overtaken us.

In the next four verses (vv. 3-6) we have a list of bodily infirmities. These may be seen most easily in the following list of phrases, with the verse location in parentheses and the phrase's probable meaning in the right-hand column.

| **Allegory** | **Meaning** |
|---|---|
| 1. "Keepers of the house tremble" (3a). | 1. The arms and hands tremble in old age with palsy or feebleness. |
| 2. "Heroic men are bent" (3b). | 2. The legs are bent in feebleness, and the knees totter. |

---

11   Delitzsch, p. 404.

| | |
|---|---|
| 3. "Grinders cease, because they are few" (3c). | 3. The teeth lose their ability to masticate food. |
| 4. "Those looking through the windows grow dim" (3d). | 4. The eyes begin to lose their sight, and the pupils become dilated and more contracted. |
| 5. "Doors on the street are closed" (4a). | 5. The lips (swinging or folding doors, as the jaws of Leviathan are called "the doors of his face" in Job 41:14) fall into the mouth for lack of teeth. (A street is cleft between two rows of houses.) |
| 6. "Sound of the grinding mill fades" (4b). | 6. In toothless old age, only soft foods may be eaten. Thus no noise is made, for no hard bread or parched corn is being chewed. |
| 7. "One rises up at the sound of a bird" (4c). | 7. The least amount of morning noise terminates sleep. |
| 8. "All the daughters of song are brought low" (4d). | 8. The qualities (daughters) that make up the power to compose and enjoy music and song elude him in his old age. |
| 9. "afraid of heights and of terrors on the road" (5a-b). | 9. He has developed a fear of heights and of stumbling along paths once familiar. |
| 10. "Almond tree blossoms" (5c). | 10. His hair has turned white with age. |
| 11. "Grasshopper drags along" (5d). | 11. The halting gait of the elderly as they walk along with their canes. |
| 12. "The caper-berry is useless" (5e). | 12. All sexual power and desire is lost. |

| | |
|---|---|
| 13. "Person goes to his eternal home and mourners go about the streets" (5f-g). | 13. This phrase can be understood naturally/literally. |
| 14. "The silver cord is severed" (6a). | 14. The spinal marrow connecting the brain and nerves is pale and silverlike. |
| 15. "The golden bowl is broken" (6b). | 15. This may be a reference to the brain because of its shape and color. |
| 16. "The pitcher is shattered at the spring" (6c). | 16. The failing heart, a pitcher-like receptacle, is pierced or broken, and all the life-supporting blood flows out. |
| 17. "The wheel is shattered at the well" (6d) | 17. The system of veins and arteries that carried the blood around continually like a waterwheel breaks down when the heart breaks. |

Then it is, after this slow dissolution has worked its evil, that the body made of earth returns to the earth (12:7). But the spirit goes to God, who originally gave it to man. In a similar expression of confidence, our Lord yielded up His life saying, "Into your hands I commit my spirit" (Luke 23:46). So said Stephen as well, "Lord Jesus, receive my spirit" (Acts 7:59). A mortal has left this earth. True, his body is still in the soil, dissolving: but it is actually—personally, and consciously—present with the Lord at that same moment.

All of this makes a person's future perilous if he does not live in the knowledge that he will soon lose the privilege of working for his Creator.

## D. 12:8-14 — Conclusion

And so our writer concludes with the theme of his prologue (1:2): "Most transitory," says Qoheleth; "all is transitory." In other words, how fleeting and shameful is it to have lived and not to have known the key to living! What a waste to have died without having enjoyed life or known what it was all about. That is the tragedy of tragedies; a great waste. By repeating the second verse of the first chapter, Solomon indicates that he has concluded his treatise and is now ready to summarize everything.

> [8]"Most temporal," says the Teacher, "Everything is temporal."
>
> [9]Besides being wise, the Teacher also taught the people knowledge; he tested and searched out, and set in order many proverbs.
>
> [10]Qoheleth searched to find the appropriate words and what he wrote were upright words of truth.
>
> [11]The words of the wise are like cattle-goads, their collections like fixed nails—given by the one Shepherd.
>
> [12]Anything more than them, my son, be warned. There is no end to the making of many books, and much study is a weariness of the flesh.
>
> [13]All has been heard; here is the conclusion of the matter: fear God and keep his commandments, for this is the entirety of a person.
>
> [14]For God will bring every act into judgment, including every hidden thing, whether good or evil.

The writer's qualifications for giving such instruction are next set forth in 12:9-10. In our judgment, this section also belongs to Solomon rather than to one of his "disciples" (as some would have it) who might have written on his behalf. The connection of verse 9 with verse 8 is clear from the conjunction "and," which begins verse 9 in the Hebrew text. The author laid claim to being "wise." Therefore his material was not the chatter of an experimenter or the musings of a "natural man." How could an unbeliever or a trifling experimenter be called wise?

Some may take exception to Solomon's calling himself "wise." But we would argue that the claim is couched in the third person instead of the first person, and the term "wise" marked him as a member of one of the three great institutions of his day: "prophet, priest, and wise man" (cf. Jer. 8:8-9; 18:18; Ezek. 7:26). The designation was a technical one, designating him as a member of the wise to whom God gave wisdom, just as the priest had the Law and the prophet had the Word. Therefore, his claim is no sign that he lacked modesty, for it is a claim that the wisdom in Ecclesiastes came from God in a revelation, just as the prophet's word also was given by divine inspiration.

Aside from the fact of his wisdom, "He continually taught the people knowledge" with a deliberateness and care that merited his audience's most serious attention: there was a careful composing, investigating, and arranging of the proverbs and lessons he wrote. This was no haphazard spouting of negative thoughts in negative language. On the contrary, Solomon deliberately searched for "pleasant words," or "words of grace" (12:10). In no way can that be a description of the work of a pessimist, nihilist, or Epicurean with an "eat-drink-and-be-merry-for-tomorrow-we-die" mentality. Few passages in the Bible tell us more about the literary method used by the writer. His description removes all doubts about alleged hastiness of thought and expression. The result of his searching for the right words was that he communicated "words of truth" and not trite remarks. He wrote in "uprightness," that is, in perfect sincerity, without any pretense.

The function and source of Qoheleth's words are next set forth in verses 11-12. The imagery is taken from pastoral life: goads (wooden rods with iron points, used to prod the oxen into action or increased speed), nails (used by shepherds to fasten their tents), and the One True Shepherd are the means Solomon uses to make his points. Accordingly, Qoheleth's words are designed to prod the sluggish into action. They "goad" him into doing something. But they are also meant to be "nails" that are "fastened" as definite points in the sluggard's mental furnishings to give him anchorage, stability, and perspective on life. At one time they are pricking his conscience, perhaps with a single proverb; at another time they are fixing themselves on the memory like a central hook on the tent's center post, which had a nail on which the important, everyday articles of clothing or cooking were kept. Some say Solomon's words are like a nail that is driven into a board to fix it in place. Those nails hold the "heads [lords] of collections" (v. 11), a reference, according to Genung, to those sayings that served as topic sentences, indicating the subject of each section or paragraph in which they stood.[12] Others (e.g., Leupold[13]) simply translate the expression as "collected sayings" to agree with the "words of the wise."

Another function found in Ecclesiastes is admonishment (v. 12). Whereas books may multiply and men may weary themselves with study of the ever-enlarging library of vol-

---

12   Genung, p. 359.

13   Herbert C. Leupold, *Exposition of Ecclesiastes* (Columbus, OH: Wartburg, 1952), pp. 296-7.

umes, the inspired words of Ecclesiastes will instruct, warn, and admonish. (The Hebrew word *zahar* does not appear in Proverbs, but it is found in Eccles. 4:13, where it means "to take advice.")

Only one true source of the book could cause Solomon, the human author, to have such a high estimation of this book of Ecclesiastes: the "one Shepherd" (12:11). This can only mean Jehovah (or, more accurately, Yahweh), the Shepherd of Israel (Ps. 80:1). He is the real source of the words of this book; not cynicism, not skepticism, not worldliness—not any of these sources. He gave the ideas, while also aiding Solomon in the composition of Ecclesiastes.

What then is the grand conclusion (end) of all these things? If we have been following our author's aim carefully, we should have added up all the parts of the preceding argument and concluded that the chief end of man is to "fear God and keep his commandments, for this is the 'manishness' of a man and 'womanliness' of a woman" (12:13). What is the "profit" of living? What does a man get for all his work? He gets the living God! And his whole profit consists of fearing Him and obeying His Word.

What is more, "every work" and "every secret deed," no matter "whether it is good or whether it is bad" (12:14), will be brought under the searching light of God's judgment in that day when all men shall personally face Him to give an account of the deeds done in the body. So echoed Paul in 2 Corinthians 5:10. Men are responsible beings, not brutes, who are destined to live to confront the past with the God that they either feared or flouted.

No formula of legalism is this "keeping of his commandments." Neither is it a method of earning favor to be used when facing God. It is a summary of the beginning, middle, and end of life as we know it on this earth: coming to know and trust the living God; receiving the gifts of life's goods; learning how to enjoy those mundane gifts; understanding the major part of the plan of God; and being guided into joyous and strenuous activity in the art of living, even while portions of life remain enigmatic.

What a book! What a good God! What a life! And what a plan!

# SELECT BIBLIOGRAPHY

Anonymous. "The Scope and Plan of the Book of Ecclesiastes," *The Biblical Repertory and Princeton Review* 29 (1857): 419-40; Also in Zuck, *Reflections*, pp. 115-31.

Anderson, William H.U. "The Curse of Work in Qoheleth: An Expose of Genesis 3:17-19 in Ecclesiastes," *Evangelical Quarterly* 70 (1998): pp. 99-113.

Archer, Gleason. "The Linguistic Evidence for the Date of Ecclesiastes." *Journal of the Evangelical Theological Society* 12 (1969): 167-81. A good but technical study.

Baltzer, K. "Women and War in Qohelet 7.23–8.1a," *HTR* 80 (1987): pp. 127-32.

Bartholomew, Craig, G. *Ecclesiastes*. Grand Rapids: Baker, 2009.

Barton, George A. *A Critical and Exegetical Commentary on the Book of Ecclesiastes*. (1908; reprinted in *The International Critical Commentary*. Edinburgh: T. & T. Clark, 1959).

Bottoms, Lawrence. *Ecclesiastes Speaks To Us Today*. Atlanta, GA: John Knox, 1979.

Breton, Santiago. "Qoheleth Studies," *Biblical Theology Bulletin* 3 (1973): pp. 22-50. A survey of most recent commentaries and studies on Ecclesiastes, not including evangelical literature.

Bridges, Charles. *Ecclesiastes*. 1860. Reprint, Carlisle, PA: Banner of Truth Trust, 1961.

Brindle, W. A. "Righteousness and Wickedness in Ecclesiastes 7.15-18," *Andrews University Seminary Studies* 23 (1985): pp. 243-57.

Caneday, Ardel B. "Qoheleth: Enigmatic Pessimist or Godly Sage?" *Grace Theological Journal* 7 (1986): pp. 21-56; also in Zuck, *Reflections*, pp. 81-113.

Castellino, George R. "Qohelet and His Wisdom," *Catholic Biblical Quarterly* 30 (1968): pp. 15-28; Also in Zuck, *Reflections*, pp. 31-43.

Christianson, Eric S. *Ecclesiastes Through the Centuries*. Oxford, UK: Blackwell, 2007.

Clemens, David M. "The Law of Sin and Death: Ecclesiastes and Genesis 1–3," *Themelios* 19 (1994): pp. 5-8.

Cox, Samuel. *The Book of Ecclesiastes with a New Translation*. The Expositor's Bible. New York: George H. Doran Co., n.d.

Crenshaw, James L. *Ecclesiastes: A Commentary*. Old Testament Library. Philadelphia: Westminster, 1987.

_____. "Qoheleth in Ancient Research," *Hebrew Annual Review* 7 (1984): pp. 41-56.

Dahood, M. "Qoheleth and Recent Discoveries," *Biblica* 39 (1958): pp. 302-18.

Davidson, Robert. *Ecclesiastes and the Song of Solomon*. The Daily Study Bible (Old Testament). General Editor, John C. L. Gibson. Philadelphia: Westminster, 1986.

Delitzsch, Franz. *Commentary on the Song of Songs and Ecclesiastes*. Translated by M. G. Easton. 1877. Reprinted in *Commentary on the Old Testament,* by C. F. Keil and Franz Delitzsch. Grand Rapids: Eerdmans, 1950. A standard evangelical work for over a century.

Donald, T. "The Semantic Field of 'Folly' in Proverbs, Job, Psalms, and Ecclesiastes," *Vetus Testamentum* 13 (1963): pp. 285-92.

De Jong, Stephan, "A Book on Labour: The Structuring Principles and the Main Theme of the Book of Qoheleth," *Journal for the Study of the Old Testament* 54 (1992): pp. 107-16.

Dreese, John J. "The Theology of Qoheleth." *The Bible Today,* November 1971, pp. 513-18. A good source of statistical studies on theological words.

Eaton, M.A. *Ecclesiastes: An Introduction and Commentary.* Tyndale Old Testament Commentaries, 16. Leicester, UK: InterVarsity, 1983.

Faulkner, R.O. "The Man Who Was Tired of Life," *Journal of Egyptian Archaeology* 42 (1956): pp. 21-40.

Fobert, Glenn. *Everything is Mist: Ecclesiastes on Life in a Puzzling and Troubled Temporary World*. Belleville, Ontario, Canada: Guardian Books, 2003. Best on the word *hebel*.

Forman, Charles C. "Koheleth's Use of Genesis." *Journal of Semitic Studies* 5 (1960): pp. 256-63. Very suggestive comparisons between the two books.

Fox, Michael V. "Qohelet and His Contradictions," *JSOT* Sup 71. Sheffield, UK: Almond Press, 1989.

_____. "Frame-Narrative and Composition in the Book of Qohelet," *Hebrew Union College Annual* 48 (1977): pp. 83-106.

_____. "The Meaning of *Hebel* for Qohelet," *Journal of Biblical Literature* 105 (1986): pp. 409-27.

Fredericks, Daniel C. *Coping With Transience: Ecclesiastes on Brevity in Life*. Sheffield, UK: JSOT Press, 1993.

_____ and Daniel J. Estes. *Ecclesiastes & The Song of Songs*. Downers Grove, IL.: InterVarsity, 2010. One of the better positive presentations of the book.

Garrett, Duane A. "The Theology and Purpose of Ecclesiastes," *Proverbs, Ecclesiastes, Song of Songs*. The New American Commentary, 14. Nashville, TN: Broadman, 1993, pp. 27-79; also in Zuck, *Reflections*, pp. 149-57.

Gault, Brian P. "What Has God Placed in the Human Heart? An Analysis of Ecclesiastes 3:11," Paper Read at ETS Annual Meeting, 15 November 2006, pp. 1-11.

Ginsburg, Christian David. *The Song of Songs and Coheleth*. 1861 Reprint. New York: Ktav, 1970. By far the most exhaustive discussion of the history of interpretation and grammatical points in Ecclesiastes.

Ginsburg, H. L. "The Structure and Contents of the Book of Koheleth," *Vetus Testamentum Supplement* 3 (1955), pp. 138-49.

Good, E.M. *Irony in the Old Testament*. Philadelphia: Westminster Press, 1965.

Gordis, Robert. *Koheleth—The Man and His World: A Study of Ecclesiastes*. 3rd ed. New York: Schocken, 1968.

Hengstenberg, Ernst Wilhelm. *Commentary on Ecclesiastes*. Translated by D. W. Simon. Philadelphia: Smith,

English, Co. 1860. An old but thoughtful Lutheran evangelical work.

Hubbard, David Allan. *Beyond Futility: Messages of Hope from the Book of Ecclesiastes*. Grand Rapids: Eerdmans, 1976.

_____. *Ecclesiastes, Song of Solomon*. Communicator's Commentary. Dallas, TX: Word, 1991.

Johnston, Robert K. "'Confessions of a Workaholic': A Reappraisal of Qoheleth," *Catholic Biblical Quarterly* 38 (1976):14-28; also in Zuck, *Reflections*, pp. 133-47.

Kaiser, Jr. Walter C., *Ecclesiastes: Total Life*. Chicago: Moody, 1979.

_____. "Integrating Wisdom Theology into Old Testament Theology: Ecclesiastes 3:10-15," in *A Tribute to Gleason Archer*. Ed by Walter C. Kaiser, Jr. and Ronald F. Youngblood. Chicago: Moody, 1986.

Keddie, Gordon J. *Looking for the Good Life: The Search for Fulfillment in the Light of Ecclesiastes*. Phillipsburg, NJ: Presbyterian and Reformed, 1991.

Kelley Michael. *The Burden of God: Studies in Wisdom and Civilization from the Book of Ecclesiastes*. Minneapolis, MN: Contra Mundum Books, 1993.

Kidner, Derek. *The Meaning of Ecclesiastes*. Downers Grove, IL: InterVarsity Press, 1976.

Krueger, Thomas. *Qoheleth: A Commentary*. Transl. O.C. Dean, Jr. *Hermeneia: A Critical and Historical Commentary on the Bible*. Minneapolis, MN: Fortress, 2004.

Kugel, J. L. "Qohelet and Money," *Catholic Biblical Quarterly* 51 (1989): pp. 32-49.

Leupold, Herbert C. *Exposition of Ecclesiastes*. Columbus, OH: Wartburg, 1952. The best of all recent attempts to interpret the book. The writer, however, yields to spiritualizing tendencies in several spots and fails to offer a coherent argument for the whole book.

Limburg, James. *Encountering Ecclesiastes: A Book for Our Time*. Grand Rapids: Eerdmans, 2006.

Loader, J.A. *Ecclesiastes: A Practical Commentary. Transl. John Vriend from Dutch*. Grand Rapids: Eerdmans, 1986.

_____. *Polar Structure in the Book of Ecclesiastes*. *BZAW*. New York: Walter de Gruyter, 1979.

Lohfink, Norbert. "The Present and Eternity: Time in Qoheleth," *Theology Digest* 34 (1987): pp. 236-40 Transl. from "Gegenwart und Ewigkeit: Die Zeit im Buch Kohelet," in *Geist und Leben* 60 (1987): pp. 2-12.

_____. *Qoheleth*. Continental Commentaries. Minneapolis, MN.: Fortress, 2002.

Longman, Tremper III. *The Book of Ecclesiastes*. The New International Commentary on the Old Testament. Grand Rapids, MI: Eerdmans, 1998.

Moore, T. M. *Ecclesiastes: Ancient Wisdom When All Else Fails: A New Translation and Interpretive Paraphrase*. Downers Grove, IL: InterVarsity, 2001.

Murphy, Roland E. *Ecclesiastes*. Word Biblical Commentary, 23A. Dallas, TX: Word, 1992.

Ogden, Graham S. *Qoheleth. Readings—A New Biblical Commentary*. Sheffield, UK: JSOT Press, 1987.

_____. "Vanity It Certainly Is Not," *The Bible Translator* 38 (1987): pp. 301-7.

Olyott, Stuart. A *Life Worth Living and a Lord Worth Loving: Ecclesiastes and the Song of Solomon*. Durham, UK: Evangelical Press, 1983.

Perrin, Nicholas, "Messianism in the Narrative Frame of Ecclesiastes," *Revue biblique* 108 (2001): pp. 51-7.

Perry, T.A. *Dialogues with Kohelet: The Book of Ecclesiastes: Translation and Commentary*. University Park, PA: Pennsylvania State University Press, 1993.

Provan, Iain. *Ecclesiastes, Song of Songs*. NIV *Application Commentary*. Grand Rapids: Zondervan, 2001.

Rainey, A. F. "A Second Look at '*amal*' in Qoheleth," *Concordia Theological Monthly* 36 (1965): p. 805.

Ricker, Bob and Ron Pitkin. *A Time for Every Purpose: Reflections on the Meaning of Life from Ecclesiastes*. Nashville, TN: Thomas Nelson, 1983.

Ryken, Philip Graham. *Ecclesiastes: Why Everything Matters*. Wheaton, IL: Crossway, 2010.

Rylaarsdam, J.C. *Revelation in Jewish Wisdom Literature*. Chicago: University of Chicago Press, 1946.

Scott, R.B.Y. *Proverbs, Ecclesiastes*. Anchor Bible. Garden City, NY: Doubleday, 1965.

Seow, Choon-Leong. *Ecclesiastes: A New Translation with Introduction and Commentary*. *Anchor Bible,* 18C. New York: Doubleday, 1997.

Shank, H. Carl. "Qoheleth's World and Life View as Seen in His Recurring Phrases." *Westminster Theological Journal* 37 (1974): 57-73. The repetitious vocabulary in Ecclesiastes is studied for possible patterns of interpretation. Also in Zuck, *Reflections*, pp. 67-80.

Shepherd, Jerry E. "The Identity of Qohelet," A Paper read at the Pacific Northwest Regional Meeting of the Society of Biblical Literature. Portland, OR: May 1998.

_____. "Ecclesiastes," in *The Expositor's Bible Commentary*. Revised Edition. Vol. 6 (Proverbs–Isaiah). Grand Rapids: Zondervan, 2008, pp. 254-365.

Swindoll, Charles R. *Living on the Ragged Edge*. Waco, TX: Word, 1985.

Viviano, Pauline A. "The Book of Ecclesiastes: A Literary Approach," *The Bible Today* 22 (1984): pp. 79-84.

Whitby, Charles F. *Koheleth: His Language and Thought*. New York: Walter de Gruyter, 1979.

Whybray, R. N. "Qoheleth the Immoralist? (Qoh. 7:16-17)." In *Israelite Wisdom: Theological and Literary Essays in Honor of Samuel Terrien,* edited by John G. Gammie. Missoula, MT: Scholars, 1978. pp. 191-204.

_____. "The Identification and Use of Quotations in Ecclesiastes," *Vetus Testamentum* Supplements 32 (1981): 435-51; also in Zuck, *Reflections*, pp. 185 -199.

_____. "Qoheleth, Preacher of Joy," *Journal for the Study of the Old Testament* 23 (1982): pp. 87-98; also in Zuck, *Reflections*, pp. 203-212.

_____. *Ecclesiastes*. New Century Bible Commentary. Grand Rapids: Eerdmans, 1989.

_____. *Ecclesiastes*. Sheffield, UK: JSOT Press, 1989.

Wright, Addison G. "The Riddle of the Sphinx: The Structure of the Book of Qoheleth," *Catholic Biblical Quarterly* 30 (1968): pp. 313-34; also in Zuck, *Reflections*, pp. 45-65.

_____. "Ecclesiastes (Qoheleth)." In *The New Jerome Biblical Commentary*. Eds. Raymond E. Brown, et al. Englewood Cliffs, NJ: Prentice-Hall, 1990.

Wright, J. Stafford. "The Interpretation of Ecclesiastes." *Evangelical Quarterly* 18 (1946): pp. 18-34. The most impressive essay to appear on this book in the twentieth century. Also available in *Classical Evangelical Essays in Old Testament Interpretation*. Grand Rapids: Baker Book House, 1973, ed. W. C. Kaiser, and reprinted in Eugene, OR: Wipf and Stock, 2008, pp. 133-150.

——————. "Introduction to Ecclesiastes," in *The Expositor's Bible Commentary*. 12 vols., Ed. Frank E. Gaebelein. Grand Rapids: Zondervan, 1991, vol. 5: pp. 1137-49; also in Zuck, *Reflections*, pp. 159-73.

Wyngaarden, Martin J. "The Interpretation of Ecclesiastes." *The Calvin Forum* 19-21 (1953-5): pp. 157-60. An interpretation that divides the book into "goads" and "nails" based on Ecclesiastes 12:11.

Youngblood, Ronald F. "Qoheleth's Dark House (Eccles. 12:5)," *Journal of the Evangelical Theological Society* 29 (1986): pp. 397-410.

Zimmerli, W. "The Place and Limit of the Wisdom in the Framework of Old Testament Theology," *Scottish Journal of Theology*. 17 (1964): pp. 146-58.

Zuck, Roy B. *Reflecting with Solomon: Selected Studies on the Book of Ecclesiastes*. Grand Rapids: Baker, 1994. A wonderful collection of the top articles on Ecclesiastes.

——————. "God and Man in Ecclesiastes," *Bibliotheca Sacra* 148 (1991): pp. 46-56; also in Zuck, *Reflections*, pp. 213-22.

**Revive Us Again**

Biblical Principles for Revival Today

**Walter C. Kaiser Jr.**

ISBN 978-1-85792-687-3

# Revive Us Again

*Biblical Principles for Revival Today*

WALTER C. KAISER, JR.

It only takes a look at the evening news for us to realize that there is much wrong with this world of ours. The sins of Greed, Lust, Violence and Corruption are rife in all sections of our society. Christians are becoming at best an irrelevance and at worst a persecuted minority. Walter C. Kaiser, Jr. suggests the one answer to these pressing problems, revival. Not a foot-stomping, soul-saving series of meetings but an individual believer's refocusing on God as the centre of life. With his usual scholarship and vision Dr. Walter C. Kaiser, Jr. reveals spiritual principles inherent in the great awakenings of the Bible and shows us how to prepare the way for revival today. Revivals like those led by Moses and by John the Baptist provide us with clear examples of what God can do when His sovereign will is acknowledged and obeyed. Read this book and help prepare the way for revival in your community, your church and most importantly your heart.

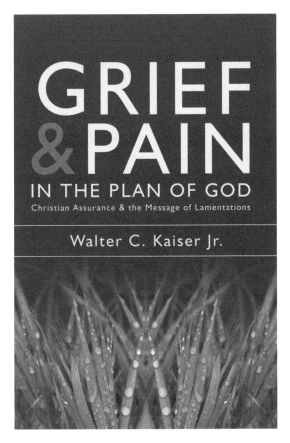

ISBN 978-1-85792-993-5

# Grief and Pain in the Plan of God

## Christian Assurance and the message of Lamentations

### Walter C. Kaiser, Jr.

Most of us will have faced that most delicate situation of meeting a person who is suffering. We tend to go down one of two different avenues. One is to offer well-intentioned advice - often in the form of well-worn cliches that the person will have heard several times before. The other is not to say anything at all - risking the danger of leaving the person under the impression that God has no idea what is going on and is unable to help.

How are we to understand suffering and its place in our lives? Should we try and rationalise it away, trying to come up with a solution that sits as comfortably as possible? Surely we should look to Scripture first? This is what Walter Kaiser does here. Looking at the Old Testament book of Lamentations Kaiser does not offer any easy solutions - but rather shows us how a Sovereign and Loving God can work through even the most painful moments.

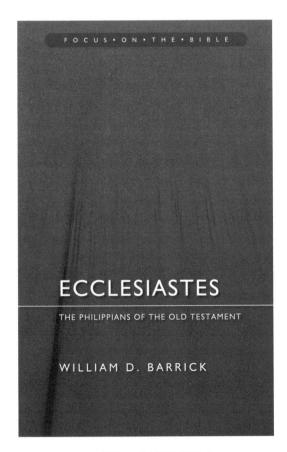

FOCUS • ON • THE • BIBLE

# ECCLESIASTES

THE PHILIPPIANS OF THE OLD TESTAMENT

WILLIAM D. BARRICK

ISBN 978-1-84550-776-3

# Ecclesiastes
## *The Philippians of the Old Testament*

### WILLIAM D. BARRICK

What is the purpose of life? The preacher in Ecclesiastes, just like many today, is in search of life's meaning. But as they look through their limited worldview all they find is "vanity, vanity". Pure emptiness! They are in search for something which will have eternal value. To find it, we need to look beyond ourselves. This is what the preacher discovers; that man is powerless, yet God has a design and purpose for all things. He is the giver of all life. Ecclesiastes gives teaching on doctrines such as man, salvation and future judgment.

William Barrick is Professor of Old Testament at Master's Seminary, Sun Valley, California. Dr. Barrick has been married to his wife Barbara for 45 years. They have four married children and fourteen grandchildren.

Colin S. Smith

# Jonah
Navigating a God-Centered Life

ISBN 978-1-84550-639-1

# Jonah
## *Navigating a God–Centred Life*

COLIN S. SMITH

Facing an assignment equivalent to being sent to warn notorious terrorists of God's anger with them, perhaps it was no wonder that Jonah ran away - certainly portrayed in Scripture as no "super saint", he avoided God and His call on his life. Yet God turned the situation around as pagan sailors encountered the living God who made the land and sea and the entire population of a city realised that although they deserved to be wiped off the face of the earth, there was a God of compassion and mercy who forgave them.

God's mercy is greater than our failures and through adverse circumstances and pain, a character of Christ-like compassion is chiselled out.

Colin S. Smith is Senior Pastor of The Orchard Evangelical Free Church in the northwest suburbs of Chicago. His preaching ministry is shared through the daily radio program, Unlocking the Bible and through his website, UnlockingtheBible.org.

Sean Michael Lucas

# Daniel
Trusting the True Hero

ISBN 978-1-84550-732-9

# Daniel

## *Trusting the True Hero*

### Sean Michael Lucas

Dare to Trust in Daniel's God! What brings you to the book of Daniel? Is it the moral example of Daniel and his robust faith? Or is it because you want to dig further into the prophetic material that speaks of the end times? Primarily the book tells you about Daniel's God. Lucas suggests rather than daring to be a Daniel, we should dare to trust in Daniel's God. This book will help you as you learn more about Daniel's God and why you too can trust him in every circumstance. Daniel was called to be a blessing even in exile and to avoid defilement in a pagan world. Such is God's call to you today so that you may honor God and put him first in your heart and life.

Sean Lucas is the Senior Minister of First Presbyterian Church, Hattiesburg, Mississippi. Prior to this, he was Chief Academic Officer and associate professor of church history at Covenant Theological Seminary, St. Louis, Missouri. He received BA and MA degrees from Bob Jones University and the PhD degree from Westminster Theological Seminary.

# Christian Focus Publications

Our mission statement –

STAYING FAITHFUL
In dependence upon God we seek to impact the world through literature faithful to His infallible Word, the Bible. Our aim is to ensure that the Lord Jesus Christ is presented as the only hope to obtain forgiveness of sin, live a useful life and look forward to heaven with Him.

Our Books are published in four imprints:

## CHRISTIAN FOCUS

popular works including biographies, commentaries, basic doctrine and Christian living.

## CHRISTIAN HERITAGE

books representing some of the best material from the rich heritage of the church.

## MENTOR

books written at a level suitable for Bible College and seminary students, pastors, and other serious readers. The imprint includes commentaries, doctrinal studies, examination of current issues and church history.

## CF4•K

children's books for quality Bible teaching and for all age groups: Sunday school curriculum, puzzle and activity books; personal and family devotional titles, biographies and inspirational stories – Because you are never too young to know Jesus!

Christian Focus Publications Ltd,
Geanies House, Fearn, Ross-shire,
IV20 1TW, Scotland, United Kingdom.
www.christianfocus.com